KINGDOM IDENTITY REALITIES

KINGDOM IDENTITY REALITIES

Sherry Brown

Trilogy Christian Publishers

A Wholly Owned Subsidiary of Trinity Broadcasting Network

2442 Michelle Drive

Tustin, CA 92780

Copyright © 2024 by Sherry Brown

Scripture quotations marked NKJV are taken from the New King James Version®. Copyright © 1982 by Thomas Nelson. Used by permission. All rights reserved. Scripture quotations marked NLT are taken from the Holy Bible, New Living Translation, copyright © 1996, 2004, 2015 by Tyndale House Foundation. Used by permission of Tyndale House Publishers, Inc., Carol Stream, Illinois 60188. All rights reserved. Scripture quotations marked KJV are taken from the King James Version of the Bible. Public domain.

All rights reserved, including the right to reproduce this book or portions thereof in any form whatsoever.

For information, address Trilogy Christian Publishing

Rights Department, 2442 Michelle Drive, Tustin, Ca 92780.

Trilogy Christian Publishing/ TBN and colophon are trademarks of Trinity Broadcasting Network.

For information about special discounts for bulk purchases, please contact Trilogy Christian Publishing.

Trilogy Disclaimer: The views and content expressed in this book are those of the author and may not necessarily reflect the views and doctrine of Trilogy Christian Publishing or the Trinity Broadcasting Network.

10 9 8 7 6 5 4 3 2 1

Library of Congress Cataloging-in-Publication Data is available.

ISBN 979-8-89333-677-1

ISBN 979-8-89333-678-8 (ebook)

DEDICATION

I dedicate this book to my heavenly Father, His Holy Son, Jesus Christ, and the Holy Spirit. They are the authentic authors of these recorded writings.

I give all praise, all glory, and all honor to them alone!

I also dedicate this book to my son, T. J. Caudill, for believing in the Spirit of God in my life and witnessing the kingdom mandate that is required of my Spirit-filled life in Jesus Christ, my Lord.

I also dedicate this book to Rob and Kristin Plumby for their unwavering faith and encouragement in this God-given dream that was spoken to me on October 6, 1986.

TABLE OF CONTENTS

Preface 9
Chapter 1: Discovering My Identity in Jesus Christ 11
Chapter 2: Set Apart unto Him 27
Chapter 3: The Throne Room Presence of Eternal Love 39
Chapter 4: Following Christ in Freedom Expression 63
Chapter 5: His Liberty Life Force 79
Chapter 6: His Supernatural Identity Manifesting
　　　　　in Our Time 89
Chapter 7: Welcome to the Suffering Side of Christ 105
Chapter 8: Knowing Jesus as a Lamb to the Slaughter 121
Chapter 9: The Supernatural Phenomena of Wisdom
　　　　　in the Heart 139
Chapter 10: A Consecrated Life unto Reverential Fear . . . 153
Chapter 11: It's God's Created Plan, Not Ours 171
Chapter 12: He Makes Full Proof of His Anointing
　　　　　 on You 185
Chapter 13: A God-Given, Anointed Dream 203
Chapter 14: Preach the Gospel in the Radiant Force
　　　　　 of Glory Fire 223

Chapter 15: Exposing Idols 241

Chapter 16: My Child, Come Up Hither 255

Closing Thoughts 273

PREFACE

Kingdom Identity Realities are the very heart of the living God and His kingdom identity realities were first birthed within the spirits of Adam and Eve in the garden as God created mankind to worship Him and to daily have intimate fellowship with Him in holiness and righteousness. This book was birthed before the throne of Grace to encourage you to step into your God-given destiny and embrace the fullness of Jesus Christ in the liberty life force of His kingdom identity that wants to take you into the depths of His throne room intimacy so you can encounter the majestic wonders of His Holy Word and supernatural nature and, in turn, give it away to souls everywhere. God wants to encourage you to live out your spiritual identity in Jesus Christ as we all are uniquely created for His holy glory, and we are not a carbon copy of another. The greatest need in the world today is the supernatural burning love of God through the salvation plan of Jesus Christ our Lord and living out our identities in Him.

Supernatural encounters are always wondrous to the heart and mind, and they help build hearts for greater discoveries in the living realities of the Spirit of God.

The supernatural realm is more real than the natural realm, as it is the divine nature of God. God is calling the whole world to bow at His footstool through the sure mercies of Jesus and know Him face to face. God will meet with you powerfully as you enter your spiritual quest of increased hunger and driven passion for the greatest force on the earth which is *love* and the security of God's authentic destiny identity for His glorious creation.

You only come along once in a lifetime, so get to know who you are in Jesus Christ.

John 4:24 (KJV), "God is a Spirit: and they that worship him must worship him in spirit and in truth."

Psalm 139:14 (KJV), "I will praise thee; for I am fearfully and wonderfully made: marvellous are thy works; and that my soul knoweth right well."

CHAPTER 1: DISCOVERING MY IDENTITY IN JESUS CHRIST

John 1:12–13 (KJV),

> But as many as received him, to them gave he power to become the sons of God, even to them that believe on his name: Which were born, not of blood, nor of the will of the flesh, nor of the will of man, but of God.

Living to Know Him

Friend, we are to be living every day to deeply know and love Him because He already knows all about us.

I was born and raised in the beautiful hills of eastern Kentucky. As my life started moving forward into my growing years, I became very interested in the supernatural, causing my heart to hunger for the great big God of the universe. My mother was a devout Christian who faithfully took me and my three brothers to church on Sundays, and she passionately taught us about God and to always dream big in Him. Oh, how I remember her sweet voice singing "Amazing Grace" and many other wonderful gospel songs that made me think about the place some called "their heavenly home." I would ponder many times throughout my young years about the mysteries of God and how He created this beautiful world for all of us to enjoy, and with each thought, my imagination became greatly enlarged!

I thought to myself many times about how I wanted to be saved, but not until I became an adult, and that was exactly what I chose to decide. I remember in those tender years being so afraid of storms with the majestic sounds of thunder and the mighty claps of piercing lightening to the point I would pray and ask God not to allow the end of time to come until I was saved, for you see, my friend, I was developing a sense of reverential fear that would strongly be with me even to this day! I always had a strong sensitivity to the Spirit of God as a young child, and I felt Him with me often, but I refused His convicting power time and time again in those tender years. The thought of being saved as a child or teenager was unthinkable for me; for you see, I was deceived by Satan's blinding ways!

I would feel many times the Lord nudging my heart with the longing for His sweet salvation call, but I had to have my rebellious way over and over again. In fact, when I was in my teenage years, the Lord visited me in a powerful way on a beautiful sunny day. I was lying out in the bright sunshine, desiring the warmth of the rays of the flaming sun to penetrate my skin, and to my amazing surprise, there was a mighty presence that engulfed me. I knew immediately that it was the presence of the Lord, and He spoke of His salvation plan to me, but I readily said, "*No*. Not now, Lord. When I get married, I will give my heart to You, but not now." So, He departed from me as swiftly as He came in around me. How sad that I said no to my glorious Savior. I was taken aback by this encounter and shared it with no one because I was raised in a church doctrine where supernatural happenings such as that were not taught as a daily lifestyle in your Christian walk.

My secret was hidden deep in my heart for many years. I would ponder this encounter many times, and I knew every time it was the very presence of Jesus that came down from heaven and visited me in a profound way, but if only I had heeded His beckoning call, I would have been spared from many futuristic things that brought deep suffering to my disobedient heart! I longed to know God all my life, and I yearned for His supernatural presence. In one single day, His holy presence came flooding in like a massive tidal wave, but I was too blind to value His glorious appearing because my heart was totally darkened without the light of His radiant salvation. Time swiftly passed, and in October 1980, I got married. Within the same month, I gave my heart to the Lord at the young age of nineteen. The Lord held me to my word, and sure enough, His salvation plan moved in and set this captive free and flooded my heart with great celebration and glorious illumination that transformed my whole life and my carnal lifestyle immediately!

My life took on a whole new meaning and with the glorious kingdom of God thinking! My husband, at the time, was backslidden and running from God. Needless to say, at the time of my salvation, his reaction to my new lifestyle was a bittersweet one, for he was away from the Lord and had his sinful taste for the world. So, in a short time, even though I was high on my new life and ready to go exploring the supernatural side of life, the devil came immediately to rob me of my joyous new life in Jesus Christ, and I, too, quickly slipped back into the ways of the world, becoming very depressed and suicidal. However, during the short time of my backsliding, my heart was always illuminated with the knowledge and seriousness of my salvation call to repent swiftly and return to the master.

So, in 1982, I repented for my waywardness and rededicated my life to the Lord, but we were attending a Baptist church, where women are limited to very little freedom expressions in the gifting and anointing of Christ. So, with my lack of knowledge of the Word of God, I made plans to end it all by a self-inflicting plot to take my life, having been deceived into thinking that because I was a woman, I could not do anything for my master. All due to legalistic and traditional false teachings by the spirit of religion I had allowed myself to sit under.

One evening, all alone in my apartment in Sturgis, Michigan, I wrote my goodbye note and decided to take what I thought would be an overdose of pills. However, the quantity wasn't enough to accomplish hell's plot to destroy my life! Praise be to God!

Suddenly, I was quickened by the Holy Spirit to open my Bible, and it fell open to Psalm 34, which became one of the most miraculous chapters of my life. That very profound psalm became the psalm of my spirit-led fed life.

The first verse is my living verse to this very day, which is recorded as follows:

"I will bless the Lord at all times: his praise shall continually be in my mouth" (Psalm 34:1, KJV).

My life was restored and renewed, and the quaking of deep hunger and thirst for more of His Holy Spirit and His delivering Word became the first place in my heart and life.

I went on a spiritual quest to know the great big God in the universe, and no matter what I had to do to achieve this supernatural goal, I was going to run with its high price and pay it with my dear life! Little did I know at that time the *heavy price* has been very great and with deep suffering! My desire to fully know the Lord was my ultimate passion, and I set out with blazing faith to see this miraculous lifestyle come to glorious fruition.

Nineteen eighty-three rolled around swiftly on the calendar of life, and so did my anticipation, for more depths of spirit life were richly blooming as I was on my fiery faith journey without any invading distractions. In this glorious year of our Lord, a sudden encounter with my compassionate and loving Jesus appeared right before me while on a desperate search for such wondrous things to manifest in my saved life. So, to my amazing surprise, right before me in an open vision, was my precious Jesus, standing behind large tree branches. The leaves were the most vivid colors, along with the glimpse of the whole vision in its entirety, but I could not see His whole face, only part of it. His skin was so beautiful and radiant with such a soft look. His eyes were as the depths of eternity flowing in the endless waves of living waters rich in love and waves of power, which caused me to be unspeakable, so much so that I was speechless and captivated while I gazed upon Christ's lovely appearance. A crystal-clear tear fell down His right cheek; as it touched His radiant face, it appeared to look like a diamond with facets of rainbow colors, and its majestic glistening form so powerfully captivated me that I was completely still in that very moment in time. He began to speak to me these words, "They are not coming against you but My Holy Spirit that lives within you."

I fell head over heels in love with my blessed Savior, Jesus Christ, and I have never been the same since! My life took on a new meaning, and all things became new. The depths of love in my master's eyes were truly unspeakable and filled with eternal wisdom that left me speechless, and I felt breathless! During the time of this profound visitation, there was so much spiritual warfare attacking my life. All I had was the Word of God and the Holy Spirit walking me through these unwanted and lonely battles.

The Holy Spirit is grieved by the way people treat one another wrongfully.

My very living existence took a turn for new beginnings and grand celebration in life when I saw my Lord face to face as we were mind to mind, heart to heart, and spirit to spirit. I entered into a royal delight of grand fellowship in the blazing fire of love and partaking of His divine nature at a greater glory realm in the richness of the beautiful baptism of the Holy Spirit.

I have now tasted a whole new life experience, and my growth process began to move into the depths of supernatural accelerations of swift security and maturity in Him as many encounters were increasing in my life and spirit. I had a divine revelation of my sure foundation upon the rock, Jesus Christ Himself, and His revealing Holy Word.

I launched myself upon the altar of heaven and totally surrendered my all before the king of glory. Little did I know my spiritual quest was full of spiritual warfare and magnificent revelations in word and spirit. Not everything was a bed of roses, but a rocky road journey that was filled with sweet fellowship, abundant grace, and intimate mercy. You see, friend, I had finally stepped into my destiny identity, and no one could steal it away, and no devil could destroy it in Jesus' name! I am a destiny identity runner! The prize is for me and me alone! We all have a race to run. Our unique authenticity in Christ must be manifested in every heart that is a blood-bought child of God! May we run the race well and receive our own individual prize with clean hands and a pure heart; after all, it's the plan of heaven.

> The earth is the Lord's, and the fulness thereof; the world, and they that dwell therein. For he hath founded it upon the seas, and established it upon the floods. Who shall ascend into the hill of the Lord? or who shall stand in his holy place? He that hath clean hands, and a pure heart; who hath not lifted up his soul unto vanity, nor sworn deceitfully. He shall receive the blessing from the Lord, and righteousness from the God of his salvation.
>
> Psalm 24:1–5 (KJV)

Called to a Major Airline

The harvest field is ripe, but the labourers are few.

Matthew 9:37–38 (KJV), "Then saith he unto his disciples, The harvest truly is plenteous, but the labourers are few; Pray ye therefore the Lord of the harvest, that he will send forth labourers into his harvest."

God is looking for vessels to flow through and use mightily for His glory. God wants to richly use every available vessel to be a witness for His kingdom and point souls to the saving knowledge of Jesus Christ and His salvation lifestyle. I am so honored to be saved and a servant of the Most High God.

God called me to a major airline as a flight attendant in 1990. I was truly handpicked, and heaven sent for this enormous task, as I was chosen to take His gospel to the world in the flying battlefield and harvest field. I totally bow my knee to the king, for He alone placed me in the airline to be a light in the darkness and to encourage hearts to the highest, giving Him all the glory for every waking opportunity! I retired in May of 2019 after twenty-nine years of spanning the heavens with my precious master at my side.

Friend, my life is not my own, for I have been bought with a high price, and I love my walk with Him as I have witnessed many miracles and healings in this ministry for many years that He has entrusted to me. It is only through His intimate mercy and redeeming grace that He empowers my very next heartbeat.

Friend, there is a walking and learning journey that we are all a part of in this small place that we call the earth, and with each new heartbeat and each new day, we must seek the illumination of the Holy Spirit and His delivering truth with help to press on in the darkness and do the best we can, for one day, our crown of glory will be set aside for just our perfect ordered time.

We all know the warfare is so hostile in these last days and we must be awake and alert to the master's glory call and take His sword and use it skillfully to defeat the forces of hell at every turn. The Lord has invested eternity in our hearts, and He wants us to come alive and be wise soldiers in the great, big army of His kingdom, displaying our militant armor at every turn. You see, for some, it's been a lifelong journey of Him molding us ever so skillfully, moving us out into His perfect plan, and fulfilling His purposes through us as it has been ordained before the foundations of the earth. The only way that I can share my testimony with you today is because of His fiery Holy Spirit that has given me the hope to press into Him in the worst of times. Still, I count it all joy to pick up my cross daily and follow my king straight up to His holy hill only to find His glory light shining and moving me out into a spacious place as I say to Him with all my heart, "I'll go, Lord. Send me."

Remember, you were created for His purpose, plan, and destiny, so get up from where you are daily, rise, and build, for the day is coming when no man can work.

Do not limit God in your life, for He alone is your guiding light and sustaining refuge in this troubled world of fallen mankind. Take His hand today, and He will walk you on a straight path of faith, hope, and love, and at the end of your life's journey, He will say to you, "Welcome in, thou good and faithful servant."

Matthew 25:21 (KJV), "His lord said unto him, Well done, thou good and faithful servant: thou hast been faithful over a few things, I will make thee ruler over many things: enter thou into the joy of thy lord."

Feed My Sheep

Another sudden moment blazed before me in 1995. A powerful and very overwhelming visitation of the Lord's Holy Spirit came all around me and spoke to me three times to feed His sheep, and O how I remember an urgency that flooded my vessel with the fiery power of His tangible anointing. I said some things to Him, and then I swiftly said, "Yes, I will feed Your sheep."

The Holy Spirit is so powerful, leaving us breathless at times. I was doing much ministry during this time without man-made papers. True ordination is of the Spirit of God and His beautiful anointing and not that of the command of man or woman.

Later, I became an ordained minister. I am so amazed at how the anointing of the Lord moves in the lives of yielded vessels and brings us into His mighty quaking and awakenings! Friend, when the Lord spoke to me to preach His Word, I was blown away at this glorious encounter, but I knew no matter the cost, I had to obey, and that is just what I did, for I had no option but to surrender to my destiny at that God moment in time and say yes, "So be it unto me according to Your Word." Those words rang the sweet sound of freedom in my soul as I was lifted into a beautiful and tangible place of a supernatural launching pad of resounding liberations in spirit and in truth with my king, Jesus! OH, what kingdom bliss! Three times, I asked the Lord this, "My Lord, do You want me to feed Your sheep?" God says what He means, and He means just what He says! He knew when He created us what He was going to tell us to do. Amen.

Luke 1:38 (KJV), "And Mary said, Behold the handmaid of the Lord; be it unto me according to thy word. And the angel departed from her."

When we have supernatural encounters with the Lord, it changes our perception and our whole life as it becomes a renewed and elevated lifestyle filled with monumental and miraculous events that bring the heart into a holy hush and totally surrendered lifestyle. The straight path of an obedient servant is what we should all desire, and walk it out with 100 percent trust in God for all His leading and spiritual increase. We can freely and truly say that this life is all for the glory of God and the saving of souls!

Hearing the Voice of the Master

One Sunday morning, as I was sitting in our full gospel church, the Lord gently spoke to me and told me that He was going to put me in prison ministry. I remember thinking, how could this be? He then gently spoke these reassuring words, "Just trust Me." And I readily did so. As time passed by, on a Sunday morning, I was seeking the Lord's face, and He spoke to me to go to a particular church in another town that Sunday night. I quickly obeyed and found myself going alone to this wonderful church that I'd never been to before. I was directed by the Holy Spirit exactly where to sit, and I readily took my seat, only to find out later the gentleman who sat in front of my row was a prison chaplain at two state facilities in Michigan. While in the church service that night, I had spoken a prophetic word that brought confirmation to the leadership, and the special favor of God was set into motion. I was soon ministering in two state prison facilities in Coldwater, Michigan, for a period of over nine years. We had many miracles, and the move of the Holy Spirit was so powerful that I never wanted to leave this rich ministry atmosphere.

Media Ministry

The Holy Spirit spoke to me to leave the prison ministry because He was moving me into another arena of ministry, which later became television ministry. I had my own teaching program out of a local Christian TV station in Lansing, Michigan, for over one year. Later, the Lord spoke to me and told me to go on the radio, so I went to our local radio station in Coldwater, Michigan, and received such favor from the manager and got a fifteen-minute slot. After some time had passed, the Holy Ghost said, "Move into a thirty-minute slot," and favor came again. So, from June 2011–June 2018, I was on air all for His glory and the harvesting of souls! God also opened doors for other radio markets throughout America, which took me into over eight years and a half of Christian media platforms.

I learned very early in my Christian walk that my identity is in my heavenly Father, Jesus Christ, His Son, and the precious Holy Spirit. God alone has led me and fed me rich manna from above, keeping my heart steadfast in His agape love and my ears attending to His voice as He knows the perfect plan for obedient servanthood and daily accountability for our lives. Amen!

This book will be a fabulous journey into the heart of God and His revealing ways of spirit life and holy guidance to the point that you will be able to rise in your designed destiny, being a destiny runner with the flaming torch of secure identity in the complete liberty of Jesus Christ, your conquering Lord!

His Word and Spirit Foundation Identity

Jesus never lacked identity because He is complete perfection in His Father; therefore, let us learn and apply to our hearts the recorded and powerful truths in Matthew chapter 16. Amen.

> When Jesus came into the coasts of Caesarea Philippi, he asked his disciples, saying, Whom do men say that I the Son of man am? And they said, Some say that thou art John the Baptist: some, Elias; and others, Jeremias, or one of the prophets. He saith unto them, But whom say ye that I am? And Simon Peter answered and said, Thou art the Christ, the Son of the living God. And Jesus answered and said unto him, Blessed art thou, Simon Barjona: for flesh and blood hath not revealed it unto thee, but my Father which is in heaven. And I say also unto thee, That thou art Peter, and upon this rock I will build my church; and the gates of hell shall not prevail against it.
>
> Matthew 16:13–18 (KJV)

Peter had a revelation and word proclamation from heaven above to speak out into the atmosphere before Jesus and the surrounding hearers. The flaming force of heaven blazed his tongue with great wisdom from the heavenly Father above and it flooded the atmosphere with sacred truth that we freely read in the eternal Word of God that has been handed down from generation to generation. May we capture the words of Peter and the response of Jesus today deep within our searching hearts, allowing us to be established upon the rock of our salvation, being firmly planted and deeply rooted in the infallible Word of the living God with all assurance that we shall know Christ in sweet fellowship and intimacy. Jesus is our sweet deliverer, our rock of salvation that no one can withstand or destroy. Hell itself cannot touch the salvation life of Jesus Christ within a sold-out vessel of honor for the master's use. Oh, what rich joy, filled with great wonders of heaven as we daily step into the spiritual identity of Jesus Christ, keeping our face like a flint hard after the royal things in the blissful kingdom of God that is daily awaiting our faithful arrival before the throne room of perfection and skillful completion!

Friend, abide in His divine and holy revelations of truth so you can grow up swiftly in all pureness of heaven and keep all lying devils under your anointed feet. In Jesus' name.

Our foundation identity is in Jesus Christ our Lord; therefore, let us rejoice in the beauty of the master as He is daily molding us into the very form of His likeness and fashioning us in His royal splendor of heaven's holiness without fail.

Isaiah 50:7 (KJV), "For the Lord God will help me; therefore shall I not be confounded: therefore have I set my face like a flint, and I know that I shall not be ashamed."

Friend, when we abide in our authentic identity, we step into the realities of heaven's attributes, which takes us far beyond our finite self where we enter a glorious realm of oneness with the master and His infinite mind, wherein there is never a fleeting moment lost but where all is gained in a limitless holy fire of heart communing accelerations of great wisdom and knowledge in the mysteries of the Father. Never be ashamed to follow hard after Jesus Christ and His royal kingdom!

Remember, the scoffers will scoff, and the mockers will mock. Still, Jesus will bless and show you His blissful ways of supernatural rest in the glory of His fire life of refreshing and constant reviving so that the heart will never lack or fail to see who's the living and breathing king of glory! Oh, so strong and mighty is He! Let Him take you into the life of His fiery desire from weakness to His strength, from doubt to faith, and from glory to glory and timeless maturity, where you will never be empty of His perfection of love, and you will be fully received before His indestructible throne of grace.

Isaiah 33:6 (KJV), "And wisdom and knowledge shall be the stability of thy times, and strength of salvation: the fear of the Lord is his treasure."

Friend, a treasure found in the spirit life of Jesus, is the living Word in the authenticity of God, His Father, and His precious Holy Spirit. May we stand upon our sure foundation of righteous salvation through Jesus Christ our Lord and embark on a fiery journey in the pages of these writings that the Holy Spirit has led my heart and hands to bring rich manna from heaven to you this day in faith, hope, and love for souls to look beyond oneself in ways that cannot be uttered but freely received to embrace your own celebrated place in the life of Christ authenticity and originality so that you can be the beautiful *you* that God created *you* to be.

Jesus Christ is our rock of absolute truth, and nothing can move His solid rock truth out of a 100 percent faith-filled heart in the life of a born-again believer who knows who they are in this small and temporal world below.

Our Father loves it when we go from the salvation foundation proclamation lifestyle experience of Jesus Christ, His Son, to wholeheartedly abiding in the transforming application of His pure truth and then flowing in the demonstrations of His Holy Spirit's power, showing His radiant and holy heart to the world.

Friend, we were born to be great believers and wealthy receivers in richly achieving kingdom realities in spirit and truth for our one true spirit living God.

I want to share with all of you this kingdom of God reality that happened to me. I was going through much spiritual warfare in the early eighties, and during that time, the Lord spoke this to me, "Take your Bible and stand on it, declaring my truth into the atmosphere and put all demons to flight in the authority of Jesus Christ."

The Word of God is *all* authority over all the works and words from hell.

The Word of God is your daily authority! Confess it every day!

What a simple word, you might say. Simple is God's Word and a way for you and me every single day. Only believe!

The Word of God's foundation is all supreme and final authority; it keeps the heart burning pure and clean, placing all demons under our anointed feet. My friend, the only rightful place the devil has is being placed under your feet and eternally cursed back to hell from which he came.

Let us pray this prayer:

Heavenly Father, we love and adore You with all our searching hearts this day. We need You so desperately in every way, every day. We are living to know You intimately in supernatural ways and with freedom expressions in our surrendered vessels, laying our hearts before Your throne so that You can pour out upon us Your golden words of life, where all living things are subject to the creator. O Lord, let the sword of Your Word remove the corruption from the heart and erupt Your kingdom character within the souls globally. We must become more like Jesus Christ with every new heartbeat that is given by You and for Your glory alone. Heavenly Father, in our destiny identity quest, we gladly exercise our childlike faith, believing that we will enter into this magnificent place of spiritual wonderment with You, and as we do, You will flood our hearts with the perfect balance and righteous alignment of heaven's sustaining truth of kingdom identity revelations and piercing the heart with living realities of Your supernatural visiting nature to us, Your children. In the name of Jesus, we pray. Amen.

Faith and Word Declaration

I will live in the Word of the living God, being one with my king Jesus and heavenly Father and the revealing Holy Spirit. I will do as God has me to do, and I will speak as I am commanded by God's supreme authority. In Jesus' name.

"But he who is joined to the Lord is one spirit with him" (1 Corinthians 6:17, NKJV).

Heart Examination Question

Do you believe that God wants you to experience the supernatural in your heart and life?

If so, then start believing and receiving today with a willing mind and expectant heart.

It's that simple! Only believe!

CHAPTER 2: SET APART UNTO HIM

All for His Glory Alone

There came a defining time in my life after my glorious salvation experience in Jesus Christ when I had a profound desire to fully believe and embrace the Holy Spirit. It was to the point that I gave Him full control of my heart and life so I could richly receive His divine wisdom in the unfolding revelations and, therefore, truly accept the living reality that I was born for greatness and set apart to accomplish many amazing things for my glorious king. That defining time was my beautiful visitation from Jesus Christ in chapter one of this book.

I had another glorious encounter in the early eighties about the glory of God, and it had a very profound effect on my life. I want to share it with you. I was having a great, diligent search in the Scriptures as my hunger for God was so evident as I was having many powerful supernatural encounters in the Spirit of God. In fact, it was then that I told God that He would never allow anything to happen to me because I was so deeply close to Him and living in the Word and spirit as mighty kingdom things were manifesting in my life daily. All of a sudden, just as fast as I was speaking those very words to the Lord, a very swift experience hit my vessel. I felt myself in the spirit falling downward at a very rapid speed. I was fully aware of complete submission to the Holy Spirit and the unique force of this downward experience in the spirit. It was quite astounding, to say the least. Then, suddenly, as

I was falling into the atmosphere, the right hand of God caught me, scooping me upward as fast as my downward experience had occurred earlier.

The Lord began to speak to me these words. "Never be in pride or spiritual pride. We can never touch His glory."

God doesn't need our help, meaning human help is powerless before God. All He requires is a surrendered vessel to flow through. He alone gets all the glory. He loves to demonstrate through humble vessels. But that's just it; God is the administrator and demonstrator.

We must always keep that in mind, heart, and vessel.

Friend, you, too, were created to accomplish many things for God, and He loves to reveal His plans to the soul that diligently seeks His face, lives a life before His throne, and trusts Him to the very end. Everything God does is great; what we think is small to Him is mighty before the throne. When God spoke the world into existence in the book of Genesis, that was great.... Yes, because every word of God is great, and every work and every human born upon the face of the earth is great and mighty, and assuredly, a mighty miracle is the creation of all humanity.

Friend, why do you think the devil hates us so much that he is constantly trying to destroy all flesh and pull souls down into the darkness where he is cursed, along with all the fallen angels that fell from heaven with him? As God created heaven and Earth for His glory, so He created you for His glory and for His beautiful, rewarding story of great beauty, holy wonders, and success. The Father longs to record upon the tablet of your heart the recorded words of living and tangible realities through His supernatural and divine nature, where you can be daily so synchronized with the Father, Son, and Holy Spirit while living in your body.

Friend, I pray these writings spur you on into higher heights and deeper depths so that you can embark on your set-apart daily journey of intimacy with your master and live out your days in victory and joyous freedom.

Friend, you must fully recognize your separation unto God, as you are set apart for His glory and abiding in the love fire of His anointing and holy desires for your entire living experiences upon the earth. God has provided for you a steadfast and serious position before His face.

There is a heart action, and faith increase as we humbly surrender our free will to give our vessel wholly to the master and allow Him to completely master and pastor our fully devoted heart. It's so magnificent to embark on this holy journey of kingdom discoveries as we learn the simplicity of the words of God and His great love for us.

I want to share with you some spiritual insight that will encourage you to look beyond yourself daily and rise up in the celebrations of heaven's holy applications of wisdom, allowing God to manifest the divine attributes of heaven within your hearts. Friend, O to the throne of grace, we run where we draw from the highest educational place known to man! Let us begin by releasing our childlike faith and sit at the feasting place with a holy hush and with an anticipating heart, only open to receive the deeper things from our heavenly Father's loving and revealing heart. May we all say now that we will expect daily miracles and glory happenings from the presence of God!

Psalm 84:11 (NKJV), "For the Lord God is a sun and shield; The Lord will give grace and glory; No good thing will He withhold from those who walk uprightly."

Friend, only believe that your position within the earth is for *His glory alone*! We must never seek our own glory by being self-seeking, self-reliant, and self-centered, which produces a hard heart, causing a cold separation and stifling in the vessel against the Spirit of God due to one refusing to receive the greater depths into the Spirit-filled lifestyle and His faithful promises. Many want to have full reign over their heart and life; therefore, one will never reach their full potential in Jesus Christ.

Many years ago, the Holy Ghost spoke this word to me, "When you come to the end of self, then you will begin greatly with God."

My friend, let us begin with God, finish with God, and forever live with God! This is a Simple word, a simple choice, and a simple truth; just believe! It is God's perfect will for you. Begin in the simplicity of child-like faith and end in complete humility and righteous standing before the throne of eternal grace.

Do you truly know your identity in Christ, or is it just mere words that sound good to your ears and the hearers among you? Are you trying to convince yourself who you are? Only be convinced of who Jesus Christ is in you and demonstrate His agape love to the world. People are waiting for Christ in you as you, my friend, might be the only Jesus that some will ever see. Give Him away in compassionate heart actions, simple deeds, and powerful Holy Spirit demonstrations.

Christ will always *reveal* who you are. As God the Father revealed Christ to us so shall Christ reveal Himself through the Holy Spirit in our destiny identity to the world! Only believe! Amen.

The Lord spoke this word to me many years ago, "You do not have to prove who you are in Me, for My anointing will demonstrate who you are in Me. Only believe."

When God speaks to the heart, He speaks with the spirit of truth, as He alone is truth and is no lie. Note: See John 16:13.

Take time daily to have an ear to hear, a mind to believe, and a heart to richly receive all from God above.

Let us look at these powerful words in Matthew 3:13–17 (KJV),

> Then cometh Jesus from Galilee to Jordan unto John, to be baptized of him. But John forbad him, saying, I have need to be baptized of thee, and comest thou to me?

> And Jesus answering said unto him, Suffer it to be so now: for thus it becometh us to fulfil all righteousness. Then he suffered him. And Jesus, when he was baptized, went up straightway out of the water: and, lo, the heavens were opened unto him, and he saw the Spirit of God descending like a dove, and lighting upon him: And lo a voice from heaven, saying, This is my beloved Son, in whom I am well pleased.

God, our heavenly Father, spoke from heaven, saying Jesus Christ is His beloved Son and that He was well pleased with Him. God purposely made known to the world who Jesus was and forever will be: His beloved Son.

May we rest in the eternal Scriptures today, knowing we are children of the Most High God and that we must act like it in spirit and in truth, being fully settled in mind and heart and living as close to Jesus Christ as we possibly can! Salvation is a doorway into the desire to walk out a daily lifestyle in Jesus Christ.

May I ask you this question?

Is your heart swaying out of balance because you are not 100 percent sure of your destiny identity in Jesus Christ? The anointed one defines you in His salvation sacrifice on Calvary's cross, where He established the eternal covenant in the wealthy foundation through His unmerited favor of intimate grace; therefore, you should always be living the transformed life in the very likeness of God's dear Son, Jesus Christ, the propitiation of our sins!

"In this is love, not that we loved God, but that He loved us and sent His Son to be the propitiation for our sins" (1 John 4:10, NKJV).

In Greek, "propitiation" means "*to make favorable,*" and it refers to averting God's wrath against sinners. *Atonement in Greek: (About appeasing divine wrath)*—properly, propitious, describing God's covenant-mercy, which rescues the believer by His atonement.

Jesus Christ is our reconciliation and sweet favor, having given us access to the throne room and to be in complete freedom, providing for us the fiery throne room fellowship with our heavenly Father.

Oh, what divine favor we have through the sacrificed lamb, Jesus Christ, our high priest, who gave us the freedom place of redemption and glory realm communing realities with God our Father.

Friend, do you, as a born-again believer, truly believe that you were created to give God alone all the glory for the great things that He has done?

Friend, bringing full attention to God and staying God-focused is well pleasing to the heavenly Father. Remember, the world and the spirit of religion are always demanding attention from the heart, but God longs for the heart of man to willfully give full attention to His Spirit and Holy Word.

Choose wisely, for your life depends upon wise and healthy choices that are of God.

This is where you will know if the spirit of religion still has a squeezing grip on your heart and mind.

Friend, you can easily stand and feed in the wealth and supernatural strength of Christ's eternal glory, having your salvation experience place you on a well-balanced scale. However, to remain well-balanced daily, your lifestyle must reflect Jesus governing your life and walking it out being spirit-led, spirit-fed, and Holy-Spirit-empowered.

Remember, the scribes and Pharisees hated Jesus for His truth and His intimate walk with God our heavenly Father because they were a constant false balance. Some ministers don't teach people about the throne room fellowship and intimacy with the Father, His Son, and the precious Holy Spirit. Many are out of balance and living in unwholesome lack.

God, have mercy, and God help us. We need sound doctrine and devout ministers who speak as an oracle of heaven where the Word of God and His radiant, fiery Holy Spirit touch the heart with such power and conviction that many never want to leave the presence of God pouring out upon their hungry hearts. Living a life in check and evenly balanced in the truth of heaven and daily practicing a Spirit-filled lifestyle opens the heart up to kingdom identity realities that are obedient to a selfless life lived in God and shining forth in the golden glory realm from glory to glory in the master's plan to work for the gospel's sake and dwell in His presence so people will see your good works and glorify the Father above. This is the place, my friend, where Christ is seen within your vessel in all transparency as He is the shepherd of your heart, and He has full ownership of your soul.

Enjoy displaying His shining and transparent glory that floods your chosen vessel with high honors of authenticity that is priceless and forever known before the throne of God! Carry on, soldier, for great rewards are awaiting you in the end!

Proverbs 16:11 (KJV), "A just weight and balance are the Lord's: all the weights of the bag are his work."

Christ Liveth in Me

Friend, to identify completely in Christ is to be dead to the lust of the rotten and corrupt flesh mess and the pride of life that wars against your spirit. Allow the power of the Holy Spirit to crucify your flesh because as you are completely rooted and established in the life of Jesus Christ, you will wholly desire to live out the fullness of a resurrected life that is tried and true before the throne of grace.

Galatians 2:20 (KJV), "I am crucified with Christ: nevertheless I live; yet not I, but Christ lived in me: and the life which I now live in the flesh I live by the faith of the Son of God, who loved me, and gave himself for me."

Christ liveth in me, the eternal hope of glory that always brings a just weight and never a false balance to my searching heart. The cross was a place of death for Jesus, and as we are in Christ's resurrection lifestyle, making our lives a living sacrifice before the throne, always placing the rotten mortal flesh at His feet and its corrupt mess so that we can be in the resurrection demonstrations of victorious liberties over the fallen nature of human frailties.

Proverbs 11:1 (KJV), "A false balance is abomination to the Lord: but a just weight is his delight."

May we all make this our daily prayer. Amen.

I must decrease so that Christ can increase. O less of me and all of You, Lord. All of you, Master, who spurs the heart to live out life in righteousness, which is Your ultimate desire for Your creation.

A just weight we shall be in a well-balanced heart of holy delight.

John 3:27–36 (KJV),

> John answered and said, A man can receive nothing, except it be given him from heaven. Ye yourselves bear me witness, that I said, I am not the Christ, but that I am sent before him. He that hath the bride is the bridegroom: but the friend of the bridegroom, which standeth and heareth him, rejoiceth greatly because of the bridegroom's voice: this my joy therefore is fulfilled. He must increase, but I must decrease. He that cometh from above is above all: he that is of the earth is earthly, and speaketh of the earth: he that cometh from heaven is above all. And what he hath seen and heard, that he testifieth; and no man receiveth his testimony. He that hath received his testimony hath set to his seal that God is true. For he whom God hath sent speaketh the words of God: for God giveth not the Spirit by measure unto him. The Father loveth the Son, and hath given all

things into his hand. He that believeth on the Son hath everlasting life: and he that believeth not the Son shall not see life; but the wrath of God abideth on him.

The holy seal of the Word of God is His covenant word for all who will hear and adhere to it with child-like faith, burning the heart with great momentum.

A Sold-Out Vessel

A sold-out vessel before the throne of grace will always be used greatly for the kingdom of heaven.

I want to share with all of you a supernatural encounter that I had in a hotel room in Detroit, Michigan, many years ago as a new hire flight attendant with a major airline. I was seeking the Lord's face before the throne, crying out to him with my whole heart, telling Him that I wanted Him more than my very next living breath; I wanted God more than the fabulous flying career that took me to many nations across the globe. I wanted God more than all things and *above* all things in this entire world. To surrender all and daily die to my rotten flesh mess was my deep conviction and driven spiritual quest to live for God 100 percent and serve Him to the fullest, and nothing less than that period was my ultimate desire in life. I was fully determined to carry out His plan for my life, no matter the cost! I truly mean literally, *no matter the cost*!

A weak moment hit my heart, and I began to tell the Lord in that brief and fleeting moment to take the ministry; all I wanted was to please Him, and I craved His presence above ministry, for you see, friend, the Lord also spoke to me that we must want His presence above all ministry and everything else in the earth. Many people are so busy doing things for God that they are missing out on being with God and His holy presence.

Friend, God's presence is all that matters, and His heart's desire is for you to spend quality time with Him, knowing full well that greater depths of love and wisdom will grow you up into a wise servant in full stature for the glory of God.

The Lord spoke to me as my whole heart was crying out for His presence. These beautiful words flooded my heart with such a tangible touch; He said, "My child, when a *whole heart* is laid before My throne in total surrender, I can do nothing but use that heart greatly for My kingdom's splendor. Now, get up from where you are, go dry your tears, and wash your face."

I fully obeyed, and my hotel room was totally engulfed with His ever-abiding presence of perfect love and holy truth. At that very moment in time, I knew I was destined for even greater things in the Spirit of God. I had many encounters with the Lord, and with each one, I was aware of the fact that I was chosen by him in a very miraculous way, also knowing that few would ever understand me in my unique walk with God because of the revelation of the strong anointing and the high price that I would constantly have to pay. I was truly set apart for the glory of God and end-time ministry for the harvesting of souls, but it also made me more of a target for the attacks of hell against my life on multiple fronts. The sweet pleasures of living in total surrender before the throne were my designed destiny celebration in true worship. God's supernatural nature and His Holy Word burn a revival fire in a humble vessel for the world to see burning ever so powerfully for Jesus Christ, our glorious king. Remember, ultimate humility gets the golden kingdom abilities before the throne!

My layover hotels globally, for over twenty-nine and a half years, provided glorious throne room fellowship realities with my holy king as the complete solace and tranquil time with the diligent Word of God search and spiritual intimacy that was my sacred lot! Oh, how I love my alone time with Jesus. We all need our alone time with the master. I pray you, too, have glorious times of holy fellowship with Jesus. It's your destiny identity in Him as He is a spiritual being, so are we spiritual beings living in a physical body on Earth.

Friend, I want to share these words with you today. The Lord spoke these words ever so gently to me many years ago, and I pray they encourage your heart as they did mine as well. For many years, I was wretched, cold, and blind, utterly refusing my master's beckoning call. I did not know the light of my Savior's redeeming covenant, and then, one glorious day, His saving Holy Spirit came into my heart to stay. All darkness and deep gloom were cast away all because of the power of his sustaining love. Into the light of His glory, I did run. Only to find the escaping place of eternal grace. His brilliant light of salvation and truth transformed my dark heart, and all things became brand new.

Now, I live under his glorious shadow, which outshines the noonday sun, and He alone enlightens my heart with cloudless wisdom and perfect knowledge that no other can ever recreate. There is never an overcast day with the king of glory leading my way! He makes all my days brighter and my spirit is always praising His glorious name!

All shame and guilt are gone because the Son of righteousness always shines His radiant truth and life within my saved vessel! Out of the darkness I have come, only to stay in the light of His perfect love, which forever shines eternal glory in my saved heart! Jesus Christ warms my heart with His love from above and keeps me shining from glory to glory as I walk in the light of His obedience. Going forth conquering opposition and devils through the power of His resurrected Son and victorious righteous story!

Let us pray this prayer:

Heavenly Father, we worship You with our whole hearts and whole vessels, giving You all the glory for the great things that You have done. We refuse to touch Your glory as we acknowledge that we are Your creation, and we choose to allow You to flood our humble vessels with Your fiery presence of holy love and holy ways of righteous living in every awakening day. Oh, master, as born-again believers, we are set apart for Your glory alone; therefore, we ask for help and divine guidance in Jesus' name to rise-up in the wisdom of heaven so that we can walk out our designed destiny in the faith, hope, and love that only come from You above. We know that You love to see us grow, glow, and go in the power of Your witnessing might to the world, burning with Your love fire desire to see souls globally saved and set free for Your glory. In Jesus' name, we pray. Amen.

Heart Examination Question

Do you believe that you can be more than you ever dreamed and that God wants you to be all that He has created you to be?

My friend, only believe, and you shall see the glory of God overtake your saved and humble vessel. It is truly that simple....

Faith and Word Declaration

We rise this day in the anointing of heaven, knowing that we are set apart for the glory of God, and we will humbly do the works of Jesus Christ our Lord in the wisdom that comes from above and displays the agape love of heaven to souls globally. In Jesus' name.

John 15:19 (KJV), "If you were of the world, the world would love its own. Yet because you are not of the world, but I chose you out of the world, therefore the world hates you."

CHAPTER 3: THE THRONE ROOM PRESENCE OF ETERNAL LOVE

Jeremiah 33:3 (KJV), "Call unto me, and I will answer thee, and show thee great and mighty things, which thou knowest not."

In this chapter, I want to share with you some of the revelation wisdom that I experienced in my throne room encounter with my heavenly Father in the early 1990s. I pray that you draw spirit life and experience a more intimate yearning to know God deeper in the glory of His all-consuming presence. Remember, it is your holy inheritance through Jesus Christ our Lord.

Friend, I had a supernatural throne room encounter with the Lord that I want to share with you. I pray it moves your spirit and stirs your heart to come up higher in your faith and soar upon the heights of the supernatural beauty of God's majestic wonders, leaving your humble vessel overtaken with the supernatural realities of Jesus Christ manifesting powerfully.

I was seeking the face of God, crying out to Him with my whole heart, desiring all that He would allow me to obtain in this life. Suddenly, I found myself engulfed by His holy presence. I was fully aware of the twenty-four elders seated around the throne of intimate grace; however, I could not see the actual throne room, but I knew in the Spirit of God that I was there having this supernatural encounter. I was fully aware of angels being there and the living creatures before the throne as well. I found myself instantaneously on my face before God, and the fire of His presence brought a depth of ultimate surrender to the point that I could only say *"yes"* to His supreme will, and then I had a divine revelation of a mighty mandate to be a witness to the multitudes and teach them the treasures of heaven in Word and Spirit!

My heart felt as though it would just explode due to the amount of weeping and being so caught up in this out-of-this-world experience, literally, although I knew I was lying on my living room floor when this encounter took place.

My heavenly Father spoke powerfully within my vessel these words, "You live in the throne room presence of My eternal love, and this is where some others live." He began to speak to me certain servants' names that I had recognized. I told Him that I wanted to be used greatly for His kingdom, and He said, "You must be crushed; it is the final phase."

My spirit was so engulfed with such glory of heaven that I spoke back to Him and told Him I didn't like being crushed, but as He already said, you must be crushed; it is the final phase. He crushed me for His glory and holy desires. Our heavenly Father loves for us to be with Him in His throne room presence of eternal love!

Friends, in the crushing, you will learn the depths of your kingdom identity and other profound things, but you must allow God to have the whole you and nothing less. There is suffering and beauty in the crushing.

In the process of crushing, there is a hushing of stillness where the still waters run deep in the soul, leaving you in the perfect flow of God's designed will. The breath of life will spring up in your thirsty soul the knowledge to allow our heavenly Father to reveal His heart to us in a very simple yet very profound way.

The heart of the Father is burning for you! Only believe!

The beauty in the crushing is that you will be greatly transformed with the mighty increase of His sacred anointing upon your life!

His Throne, My Eternal Home

Hebrews 4:16 (KJV), "Let us therefore come boldly unto the throne of grace, that we may obtain mercy, and find grace to help in time of need."

There is a place where we can go; it's a place that soothes the aching soul; it is the throne of grace, the place of eternal escape.

Our heavenly Father loves a humble heart that is consumed with His throne room presence of revival fire, which births a magnitude of spiritual success with kingdom qualities that are produced in the obedient heart of the servanthood lifestyle of Jesus Christ Himself.

In my throne room encounter, I was fully engulfed with such holy surrender that my very nature was of the supernatural nature of His celestial Spirit life. I had a profound revelation that this glorious place was most holy and was an all-life-staining living room of greatness and holy phenomena that could only be revealed as God permitted. God's merciful love was all-consuming, and I knew I was in covenant with the creator of heaven and Earth! His merciful heart of love began revealing wisdom that overtook me with a sense of wonderment, so much so that I fully comprehended that I would one day record it in a book and share it with others so that they, too, could learn how to dwell in the throne room presence of His consuming fire and captivating love. We must daily live before the throne and feast upon the rich manna of heaven's delicacies. Many souls are desperate for the pure truth and the spiritual realities of heaven in our saved hearts as born-again believers. God wants us to be His witnesses to a lost and dying world so that we can enjoy life for eternity before His ever-abiding presence.

The most powerful and sustaining place to arrive daily is at the eternal throne of grace, which is when you know you have *arrived* because, at the throne, there is love, mercy, and grace. It's a place of repentance and calling upon God for help and guidance for daily living. All supernatural means for living a fully victorious and sustained life are all-encompassing at the throne of intimate grace.

His throne is my eternal home and eternal destination, and it is available for all who repent of their sins and ask Jesus Christ to come into their hearts forever to stay as they live for Him in complete surrender. His throne is our forever home. Amen.

The earth is not our eternal home, nor can it be. It is a temporal place for our preparation to be ready to meet God face to face and live with Him in heaven for all of eternity. When we dwell in homes built by man's hands, we can enjoy them for a short time as life is but a vapor.

James 4:13–14 (KJV),

> Go to now, ye that say, To day or to morrow we will go into such a city, and continue there a year, and buy and sell, and get gain: Whereas ye know not what shall be on the morrow. For what is your life? It is even a vapour, that appeareth for a little time, and then vanisheth away.

James reminds us how short our lives are on Earth, and he records it for us to read and live by.

It is imperative that we seek the face of God to know His heart and to serve Him wholeheartedly while there is still breath within our bodies. God longs for us to come before His presence and draw as much Spirit life and truth from Him as we can. It's His perfect will to fellowship and become close to us in our diligent search to commune with Him.

> My little children, these things write I unto you, that ye sin not. And if any man sin, we have an advocate with the Father, Jesus Christ the righteous: And he is the propitiation for our sins: and not for ours only, but also for the sins of the whole world. And hereby we do know

> that we know him, if we keep his commandments. He that saith, I know him, and keepeth not his commandments, is a liar, and the truth is not in him.
>
> 1 John 2:1–4 (KJV)

When we keep His commands and desire to deeply know His holy heart, His Word must always be the first place in our hearts and lives because His Word is His heart, and in keeping His commands, our growth accelerations will be radiant in His manifested glory. We are a shining light in the darkness, as the devil knows that.

> God, who at sundry times and in divers manners spake in time past unto the fathers by the prophets, Hath in these last days spoken unto us by his Son, whom he hath appointed heir of all things, by whom also he made the worlds; Who being the brightness of his glory, and the express image of his person, and upholding all things by the word of his power, when he had by himself purged our sins, sat down on the right hand of the Majesty on high.
>
> Hebrews 1:1–3 (KJV)

The Inner Chamber of His Heart and Growth Process of Accelerations

Song of Solomon 1:4 (KJV), "Draw me, we will run after thee: the king hath brought me into his chambers: we will be glad and rejoice in thee, we will remember thy love more than wine: the upright love thee."

Into the bridegroom chamber of the Father's fiery heart, we run today to meet with Him face to face, heart to heart, mind to mind, and spirit to spirit. We bow down in the action of total surrender at the throne of grace daily, and as we do, the flaming force of God's consuming fire pours over our empty vessels the heavenly attributes that open our hearts to the ways of profound intimacy and stirs our vessel to hunger with the deepest of yearnings so that we will continually long to stay in a place of great education for daily supernatural manifestations within us, the bride of Christ.

Run into the inner chamber of His heart where there is no danger but only His creative work of art creating within the heart His divine nature of authenticity and holy accountability.

In my throne room encounter, I felt the majestic accelerations in the blessing of obedience before our Holy Father! Be quick to obey Him today so you can accelerate in the rewarding power of limitless obedience.

The kingdom of God is a growth process of deep accelerations of truth partnered with child-like faith, leaving the heart in a wondrous state of burning in the growing desires that are well pleasing to our heavenly Father because His very heart is promoting our obedience in this acceleration place!

In the inner chamber depths of the Father's heart, the complete surrender burns with the fire of constant growth, keeping the love fire burning for the mighty revival of deeper hunger and thirst for truth upon truth and the process for the greater depths of holiness are for us to encounter.

Matthew 5:6 (KJV), "Blessed are they which do hunger and thirst after righteousness: for they shall be filled."

His Throne Room Intimacy

Song of Solomon 2:10 (KJV), "My beloved spake, and said unto me, Rise up, my love, my fair one, and come away."

Embrace the intimate fellowship place this new day in a mighty way! I love the intimacy with God the Father, and seeking His heart is a royal delight because it imparts His kingdom qualities to our searching vessels so that we can richly impart and impact others with the glorious experiences that we obtain. Oh, to know Him in the eternal breath and intimate depths of His burning love is our quest as we abide upon this temporal earth each day, knowing that there is so much more that is calling our hearts far away into the wealthy kingdom identity lifestyle of new hope in the supernatural spirit flow of heavens beckoning shore. May we still our hearts and settle our minds today in the high life of God's glory rush of radiant light in the unfolding pages of His comforting words of life. His words give us new hope that blooms a greater manifestation of unspeakable happiness in our earthen vessels. My friend, as we are daily maturing in the Word and Spirit of God, we hunger and thirst for even more of the Lord's presence, with the longing for intimacy burning its passion deep within our hearts. So, we do rush into the heavenly Father's welcoming chamber this day only to find Him with open arms and flaming love that consumes our hearts in the blazing passion of the Holy Ghost's drunkenness of glory to glory, the increased life in word and spirit. He is calling His bride away into sweet Holy Ghost fire intimacy every day.

The Word of God is our intimate desire, rising daily and applying its compelling pages to our hearts. The Lord loves to say, "Come away with me."

His Holy Love Fire Desire

Isaiah 45:3 (KJV), "And I will give thee the treasures of darkness, and hidden riches of secret places, that thou mayest know that I, the LORD, which call *thee* by thy name, *am* the God of Israel."

The holy fire of God is a blazing force of resounding power. God's Holy Spirit's fire opens up one's heart and deposits the ministry's desire of wise kingdom treasuries within the vessels of humility, and it is a continued cycle of glory to glory, meaning ever increase and elevating with jubilant acceleration!

In my throne room encounter, I experienced great crushing, and the force of God's divine nature stilled my vessel with a holy hush. In this supernatural quaking and awakening of tangible glory life, I found myself with the depository of heaven's ministry treasury of great abundant overflow, which was the Father's heart being revealed unto me concerning the ministry depths of His holy desire to educate and bring a fiery *hope* to the hungry and thirsty multitudes. I know that my encounter was for the ministry of others, and the simplicity of my teachings would encourage many to move out into their designed destinies where they could reach their full potential in Christ and be fulfilled within their own dusty frames! His holy love fire desire is the great commission and steadfast mission to win the lost at all costs! What hidden riches of an endless treasure trove of glory wonders for us to behold! What sacred secrets are our healthy inheritance.

The Beauty of Stillness

Psalm 46:10 (NKJV), "Be still, and know that I am God; I will be exalted among the nations, I will be exalted in the earth!"

Friend, God loves it when we are still before Him and completely trusting Him for everything concerning our lives. He loves it when we pay full attention to Him. Jesus Christ's burning desire is to reveal the Father's heart and guide us safely in the paths of righteousness and supernatural experiences.

We must fully know that God wants the best for us. Amen.

In my throne room encounter, I knew that God required my stillness as I was blissfully experiencing a supernatural rest that I had not experienced before. I felt this supernatural rest was not of the world, and that was so overwhelmingly evident. I had a knowledge of the importance of resting in the Spirit in the throne room. I love that we can be so still and greatly thrilled with the presence of God, which burns so deeply within our saved hearts.

In the beauty of stillness in the Spirit, there is a holy hush that soothes the heart with the anointing on high and blazes pure wisdom, depths of security, and peace deep within the sold-out vessel. One can only stay captivated in the glory realm of heaven's holy education. The all-surpassing peace of Jesus Christ burns the blessed hope in hearts that want to taste the goodness of God in His divine revelations at every given opportunity.

Our Wealthy Inheritance

> For this is the covenant that I will make with the house of Israel after those days, saith the Lord; I will put my laws into their mind, and write them in their hearts: and I will be to them a God, and they shall be to me a people.
>
> Hebrews 8:10 (KJV)

We are covenant recipients of Christ's blood covenant and inheritance through His death on Calvary. Heaven's wealthy inheritance is living in our hearts, so richly enjoy it, for it cost Jesus Christ everything!

Hebrews 7:22 (KJV), "By so much was Jesus made a surety of a better testament."

Revelation 5:12 (KJV), "Saying with a loud voice, Worthy is the Lamb that was slain to receive power, and riches, and wisdom, and strength, and honor, and glory, and blessing."

Friend, the very seven spirits in Revelation 5:12 that were the attributes of Christ have given us the access and full inheritance in Him to receive His glorious kingdom attributes and abide in the kingdom fiery chamber of our Holy Father's heart and carry His eternal designed identity destiny of glory wonders within our saved and sold out vessels that belong completely to our heavenly Father! The Lord said, "I have given you your holy inheritance now. Don't ever throw it away."

In my throne room encounter, I was resting in the blissful knowledge that we have this sacred lot through the blood covenant of Jesus, which is this: We have the purchased access to know the very heart of God, and in knowing Him, we have the grand opportunity to give it away to hearts around the globe every day! Our wealthy character in Christ will never be thrown away but forever before the throne to stay! No wealth in this *world* can ever touch the holy inheritance that is alive in our saved hearts! Each one of us has a mandate to fulfill, and God has given us all a blueprint of creative design that will empower us to impact the world for His glory and His alone. Therefore, we must adhere to His beckoning call and run to the ripe harvest field with wealthy, seasoned words that build hearts for greater hunger and supernatural demonstrations of power and kingdom identity realities. We are assigned to souls globally for the gospel's sake.

My friend, we have a holy inheritance in Jesus Christ our Lord that belongs to every born-again child of God, and we freely, through Jesus our Lord, can access the wealth of it so that we can obtain a day-to-day fulfilled life in spirit and in truth.

I want to share with you about another encounter that I had with my master to help you embrace your fully inherited place before the throne of grace and the treasure trove of timeless promises that empower the heart to walk in the divine revelations of supernatural manifestations of God's intimate glory wonders.

I had a glorious encounter with the Lord back in the 1980s that I want to share with you today.

I was going through some intense spiritual warfare at the time, and the Lord was teaching powerful biblical principles of my kingdom inheritance in His Holy Word and how to apply them to my life, as well as exercising the declarations of authority in Jesus, my Lord and king.

The Lord began to speak these words to me, "The blood of Jesus covers this house." Then, He had me march around my dining room table *seven* times, declaring into the atmosphere that *the blood of Jesus covers this house*. He then said, "Now, count the words," and they were seven as well. He reminded me of the story about Joshua marching around Jericho seven times on the seventh day, and the wall fell down and they took the city. Only Rahab, the harlot, lived and all that was with her in her house. God gave me the victory over all the powers of the enemy in that battle as well. My friend, what belongs to the Lord is His, and what He gives to us as an inheritance only through the blood of Jesus, His resurrected Son.

> Now Jericho was securely shut up because of the children of Israel; none went out, and none came in. And the Lord said to Joshua: "See! I have given Jericho into your hand, its king, and the mighty men of valor. You shall march around the city, all you men of war; you shall go all around the city once. This you shall do six days. And seven priests shall bear seven trumpets of rams' horns before the ark. But the seventh day you shall march around the city seven times, and the priests shall blow the trumpets. It shall come to pass, when they make a long blast with the ram's horn, and when you hear the sound of the trumpet, that all the people shall shout with a great shout; then the wall of the city will fall down flat. And the people shall go up every man straight before him." Then Joshua the son of Nun called the priests and said to them, "Take up the ark of the covenant, and let seven priests bear seven trumpets of rams' horns before the ark of the Lord." And he said to the people, "Proceed, and march around the city, and let him who is armed advance before the ark of the Lord." So it was, when Joshua had spoken to the people, that the seven priests bearing the seven trumpets of rams' horns before the Lord advanced and blew

the trumpets, and the ark of the covenant of the Lord followed them. The armed men went before the priests who blew the trumpets, and the rear guard came after the ark, while the priests continued blowing the trumpets. Now Joshua had commanded the people, saying, "You shall not shout or make any noise with your voice, nor shall a word proceed out of your mouth, until the day I say to you, 'Shout!' Then you shall shout." So he had the ark of the Lord circle the city, going around it once. Then they came into the camp and lodged in the camp. And Joshua rose early in the morning, and the priests took up the ark of the Lord. Then seven priests bearing seven trumpets of rams' horns before the ark of the Lord went on continually and blew with the trumpets. And the armed men went before them. But the rear guard came after the ark of the Lord, while the priests continued blowing the trumpets. And the second day they marched around the city once and returned to the camp. So they did six days. But it came to pass on the seventh day that they rose early, about the dawning of the day, and marched around the city seven times in the same manner. On that day only they marched around the city seven times. And the seventh time it happened, when the priests blew the trumpets, that Joshua said to the people: "Shout, for the Lord has given you the city! Now the city shall be doomed by the Lord to destruction, it and all who are in it. Only Rahab the harlot shall live, she and all who are with her in the house, because she hid the messengers that we sent. And you, by all means abstain from the accursed things, lest you become accursed when you take of the accursed things, and make the camp of Israel a curse, and trouble it. But all the silver and gold, and vessels of bronze and iron, are consecrated to the Lord; they shall come into the treasury of the Lord." So the people shouted when the priests blew the trumpets. And it happened when the people heard the sound of the trumpet, and the people shouted with a great shout, that the wall fell down flat. Then the people went up into the city, every man straight before him, and they took the city.

Joshua 6:1–20 (KJV)

Friend, Joshua and his men had a great victory that day, but let's take time to look at Joshua.

Joshua operated in the fullness of obedience to God the Father and His covenant commands. Joshua lived in the fullness of his kingdom identity and holy inheritance as his wealth of the spirit realm walked him powerfully in the authority of God, marching and possessing the land as God commanded, with the ark of the covenant being carried in full victory as God told Joshua that He had given Jericho into his hands. He was a successful leader through the leading of God, and he walked in the reverential fear of God. Note: Joshua 6:27 (NKJV), "So the Lord was with Joshua, and his fame spread throughout all the country."

When we abide in our holy inheritance, we will do great exploits for God and His kingdom. *All* things are before His holy throne, and to Him belong all glory, honor, and praise! Amen.

His Glorious Touch in the Garden of His Heart

Jeremiah 31:12 (KJV),

Therefore they shall come and sing in the height of Zion, and shall flow together to the goodness of the Lord, for wheat, and for wine, and for oil, and for the young of the flock and of the herd: and their soul shall be as a watered garden; and they shall not sorrow any more at all.

In my throne room encounter, I had a rich sense of provision that moves one into the very depths of the rich manna, where a delicious feasting of sweet illumination overwhelms the vessel. The glorious touch of God was moving swiftly all around me, and the awareness of His heart was melting my vessel with the liquid fire of His Spirit life, and He spoke, "You are in the garden of My heart; take what you will and be richly fulfilled!" His supernatural love touch is for all to experience through child-like faith and simple sensitivity! When we receive His love touch and enter into the garden of His delight, we will become more fruitful and productive as the fire of hope burns greater for the young and the old.

We run with heaven's vision into the darkened world, knowing heaven's glorious touch has fully awakened us to divine alignment and new assignments!

His Majestic Crown Instead of Frail Ashes

"Henceforth there is laid up for me a crown of righteousness, which the Lord, the righteous judge, shall give me at that day: and not to me only, but unto all them also that love his appearing" (2 Timothy 4:8, KJV).

We are but dust and ashes, and He is our crowning glory lifestyle! Oh, the goodness of Christ and His victorious life force placed us in the rewarding high place of redemption and glorious celebrations of victory without end!

In my throne room encounter, I felt so crushed and lifeless, only to swiftly realize that I was not mere ashes but a beautiful vessel that had been set apart for a divine and creative work for the Father's heart, and I had a profound knowledge of just that! I felt myself in my future, even though I was lying on my face before the presence of God. I felt the levels of education pouring over me, the majestic instructions to bring greater teachings to all hearers, and the release of this profound wisdom would be for others to embark on and make a sure election into the depths of the wells of salvation and the blissful realization that the throne room lifestyle was only a heartbeat and prayer away in every unfolding day with Jesus Christ awaiting our humble arrival.

We must step into our rewarding place of servanthood daily, step out in the jubilant force of heaven's ministry desire, and do our best to compel souls to come in!

Job 23:10 (KJV), "But he knoweth the way that I take: when he hath tried me, I shall come forth as gold."

His Beautiful Ashes

Out of the ashes, I did rise.

At the breath of His Holy Spirit, my ashes turned into words of gold created for His glory.

Our flesh needs to become an ash heap, while the spirit needs to become as pure gold before his throne.

His crown of glory is our rewarding and intimate kingdom identity story. Amen!

His Supernatural Nature

Isaiah 66:1 (KJV), "Thus saith the Lord, The heaven is my throne, and the earth is my footstool: where is the house that ye build unto me? and where is the place of my rest?"

Our Father's holy presence loves to be in our presence.

The supernatural nature of God is all-consuming and all-knowing. God is bigger than anything that would come against you. He's almighty and all-powerful. We should never limit God.

In my glorious throne room encounter, I was enflamed with the manifested fire of God's presence, where He showed me the powerful victory of His presence and how heaven is His throne, and Earth is His footstool. Therefore, we are always in the presence of God, and all things are always placed under His anointed feet. All enemies of the cross are completely defeated, and our confession of unhindered faith commands it so as we speak the infallible Word of God into the atmosphere! In the wisdom of God, we reside in the conquering alignment of God's authoritative truth and light of steadfast victory. The only rightful place the devil has in your life while living on Earth is crushed under your anointed feet! Let it be so in Jesus' name today! Amen!

Friend, when you walk on the earth with Jesus Christ, you walk in the ever-abiding presence of God as you remain consecrated to Him. Many never desire to become consecrated unto God and serve Him wholeheartedly.

His Prophetic Fiery Depths

Jeremiah 20:9 (KJV),

> Then I said, I will not make mention of him, nor speak any more in his name. But his word was in mine heart as a burning fire shut up in my bones, and I was weary with forbearing, and I could not stay.

The voice of the prophetic is sometimes turned away here below and heavily persecuted without remedy, but at the throne of grace, it is the very voice of God! God has foreknowledge that is sometimes filled with mysterious wonders that constantly blaze with glorious fire like Jeremiah—the Word of God was like fire shut up in his bones!

The momentum of the heart of the prophetic is a running force of purified rewards because those that flow in the prophetic always live in the depths of suffering, but while in the depths, the fiery force of God's intimate glory burns a rushing power of constant stability that keeps the heart and mind in the perfect sync of heaven's pure flow all the time! In my throne room encounter, all prophetic wisdom flowed in harmony with the full assurance of heaven backing up all spoken words, and nothing was permitted to nullify a single promise. What God has spoken, He will make it good! Out of the depths of His heart are creative wonders that no flesh can compute.

When God gives a prophetic word, we must release it as He directs as He looks for our obedience.

His Blazing Sword of Unconquered Power

Hebrews 4:12 (KJV),

> For the word of God is quick, and powerful, and sharper than any twoedged sword, piercing even to the dividing asunder of soul and spirit, and of the joints and marrow, and is a discerner of the thoughts and intents of the heart.

In my throne room encounter, the words of God brought forth a melting force into my vessel, and I was in a place of great weeping. God's Word ran through every cell of my being, and its authoritative power impacted me with such expectancy to where I was so liberated with a real sense of wisdom and knowledge that moved me into a revolving place of rich rejuvenation so that I was fully equipped to train up others to move out in the armor of heaven and become a mighty soldier in the army of the Lord! We must be fully engaged with the militant force of God's pure truth and disengaged from the world! Amen.

Hebrews 11:1 (KJV), "Now faith is the substance of things hoped for, the evidence of things not seen."

Friend, we take our fiery faith and use it mightily with the skillful sword of the Lord, moving with the harmony of both in full synchronization as the words flow from our anointed lips, speaking life to the hearers and casting demons back to hell where they belong when need be in Jesus' mighty name.

The Lord gave me this acronym for faith: Faith Alive In The Heart.

Living in the Consuming Fire of God's Holy Presence

Hebrews 12:29 (KJV), "For our God is a consuming fire."

Friend, I had another powerful encounter with the Lord and His all-consuming eternal presence before the throne of grace. I had asked Him to burn everything out of me that is not of Him and does not bring Him glory; I wanted it all totally away from me. He burned deeply within my heart as I had asked, but He also deposits as He's removing. He spoke these words to me, "When you are before My throne, take all that I give thee, for when I'm removing things from the heart, I am also depositing great things within the heart."

I literally want nothing but His divine nature living within my sold-out vessel and His Holy Word governing my heart and life on Earth, and that is what God yearns for all His children. He does faithfully burn as we seek Him daily for the holy life available in His kingdom attributes.

Friend, the holy fire of heaven is the tangible identity of Jesus Christ, the *Word* within us speaking in the power of His Holy Spirit in the secret place of holy covenant communing with God, our heavenly Father.

My friend, our Father loves to melt the heart in His presence to the point that His all-consuming fire transforms us into the greater likeness of Jesus Christ, where we step into the earth with the blazing force of the anointing of heaven in powerful demonstrations in our Spirit-filled vessels.

His presence is the fire that transforms us into the likeness of Jesus our Lord and walks us out into the daily leading of His Holy Spirit.

Receive of My Love

John 16:27 (KJV), "For the Father himself loveth you, because ye have loved me, and have believed that I came out from God."

Friend, many years ago, I was in one of my layover hotel rooms seeking the Lord in His throne room presence. He began to speak to me words that rang so loud and *true* in my empty vessel. His voice was so powerful, to the point I had a trembling going through my body.

He said, "Get up, stand to your feet, worship Me, and receive of My love."

I did just that, with hands raised and trembling. As I was worshipping Him, His glory filled my hotel room, and I fell back upon my bed. The presence of God was astounding! He spoke again, commanding me to stand up and worship Him with lifted hands toward heaven. I did so as I was still trembling, and the power of His presence came, and I fell upon the bed a second time. I literally could not stand in the presence of God. I was so in awe and utterly speechless by this encounter.

To my amazing surprise, a third command came from the Lord, as was the first two. He spoke again, commanding me to get up, stand up, and worship Him with lifted hands toward heaven. I did so as I was still trembling, and the power of His presence came, and I fell upon the bed for the third time.

I was so consumed by His holy love fire that I could not express its supernatural nature even if I wanted to; all I could do was experience it. Oh, the glory of His presence is what we must seek with all our hearts!

God loves people. He has invested eternity within their searching hearts!

My friend, on this particular day, I learned a valuable lesson that is at the forefront of my heart and mind: God loves me, and He loves you, and He wants all of His creation to receive His eternal love that knows no bounds. He loves with everlasting love, and that very love is the holy force of His radiant presence that delivers all hearts from the darkest sin and lowest place!

My friend, I ask that you allow God to love you and show you His Son's salvation, and then you will enter the spiritual light of higher living before the throne of grace. The highest place is the throne of eternal grace.

Friend, God so loved you, and He sent Jesus to save you and show you His heart, allowing you to inherit the kingdom of God in all its glory. Amen. Note: John 3:16.

Friend, you must only believe the Word of God and receive it in your heart.

We simply cannot fully explain the Holy Spirit; we have to experience the Holy Spirit's power. Amen!

> But God demonstrates His own love toward us, in that while we were still sinners, Christ died for us. Much more then, having now been justified by His blood, we shall be saved from wrath through Him. For if when we were enemies we were reconciled to God through the death of His son, much more, having been reconciled,

> we shall be saved by His life. And not only that, but we also rejoice in God through our Lord Jesus Christ, through whom we have now received the reconciliation.
>
> Romans 5:8–11 (NKJV)

I always say God loves us in spite of us, and that is good news!

We become born again to be saved and deeply changed; we do not change and then become born again. The fallen nature of an unsaved soul is lost in the total darkness of sin and in need of repentance, redemption, and glorious transformation! We embrace and receive our heavenly Father's love today in child-like faith, stepping into the merciful power of our master, who makes us worthy to be in covenant with His Father.

God walks us through flames of agony without fail. He is here for us, and He defeats all the attacks of hell on every side. His love is faithful.

Romans 8:35 (KJV), "Who shall separate us from the love of Christ? shall tribulation, or distress, or persecution, or famine, or nakedness, or peril, or sword?"

> As it is written, For thy sake we are killed all the day long; we are accounted as sheep for the slaughter. Nay, in all these things we are more than conquerors through him that loved us. For I am persuaded, that neither death, nor life, nor angels, nor principalities, nor powers, nor things present, nor things to come, Nor height, nor depth, nor any other creature, shall be able to separate us from the love of God, which is in Christ Jesus our Lord.
>
> Romans 8:36–39 (KJV)

God's love knows no end,

It reins His glory in you from heaven above

O faithful, just, and true is the Father's love toward you.

What great mercy and intimate grace

Burns in His heart never to depart,

His love fire that seeks to deliver and save

Is at His right hand

And speaking your precious name.

Receive of His love today

And ask Jesus to save your soul

For then, you will be adopted into the sheepfold.

Carrying in your vessel His love for all mankind.

Christ in you, the hope of glory

Christ in you, your identity destiny

And kingdom realities.

We are not our own; we have been bought with a price. We are prisoners of Jesus Christ! I asked the Lord many years ago what that meant to be a prisoner of Jesus, and He spoke these words, "I alone hold the key to your heart."

Glory be to God in the highest as the joy runs deep in my soul!

Apostle Paul writes that he was a prisoner of Christ Jesus, which is a beautiful and powerful lifestyle that's not of this fallen world, nor will it ever be.

Philemon 1:1 (KJV), "Paul, a prisoner of Jesus Christ, and Timothy our brother, unto Philemon our dearly beloved, and fellowlabourer."

For many years, I was wretched, cold, and blind, utterly refusing my master's beckoning call. I did not know the light of my Savior's redeeming covenant. Then, one glorious day, His saving Holy Spirit came into my heart to stay.

All darkness and deep gloom were cast away all because of the power of His sustaining love. Into the light of His glory, I did run. Only to find the escaping place of eternal grace. His brilliant light of salvation and truth transformed my dark heart, and all things became brand new.

Now, I live under His glorious shadow, which outshines the noonday sun, and He alone enlightens my heart with cloudless wisdom and perfect knowledge that no other can ever recreate. There is never an overcast day with the king of glory leading my way! He makes all my days brighter, and my spirit is always praising His glorious name!

All shame and guilt are gone because the son of righteousness always shines His radiant truth and life within my saved vessel! Out of the darkness I have come, only to stay in the light of His perfect love, which forever shines eternal glory in my heart!

Jesus Christ warms my heart with His love from above and keeps me shining from glory to glory as I walk in the light of His obedience. Going forth conquering opposition and devils through the power of His resurrected Son and victorious story!

Friend, it's a wonderful life receiving the Father's love and believing His living Word that takes us out of self so we can begin greatly in His kingdom lifeways!

CHAPTER 4: FOLLOWING CHRIST IN FREEDOM EXPRESSION

Follow Me, Follow Me

My friend, there are many expressions of Christ's holy freedom to usward on the earth, and I want to share these very special ones with you in this chapter.

My friend, I want to share with you an encounter I had with the Lord years ago.

I had an open vision that Jesus Christ was walking on a dusty path, which was leading slightly up a small hilly area. He was wearing what appeared to be a heavy woven robe in the colors of beige and a thin brown stripe; He was also wearing sandals. As He gently walked in front of me, He placed His left hand on a stone wall that was made with many different-sized stones, and how glorious for me to behold such a beautiful and captivating experience that pleased my eyes and heart with rushing wonders of His greatness gently moving along in front of me. As I was following closely behind my master, He slowly placed His left hand on top of the constructed stone wall that appeared to be so ancient, and I knew the setting of this vision was in the Middle East. His robe was flared out at the wrist, and I was so engulfed with my eyes being so focused on how He ever so gently touched the top of the wall, which seemed to be about the waist height of stature.

The left hand of the Lord would raise up a bit and gently drop down on the wall and repeat the motion as we kept walking forward. I didn't see His face, but we had a beautiful time in the vision as I was solely focused on following Him completely. I knew that He was so happy that I was following close behind Him without any distractions of any kind. I was completely smitten by the presence of my master leading me, and He desired that nothing would ever pull my heart away from His Spirit-led ways.

In this glorious vision, the sun was so brightly shining, and the somberness of this fallen world was nowhere to be found. It was as if all that was upon the earth was me and Jesus, my Lord, dressed in a shepherd's robe with skillful and supreme qualities that displayed a heavenly descent that could never be touched by a human, Lucifer himself, or his fallen demons. To follow Christ is to follow eternal destiny in fulfilled completion. The Lord always gives special attention to His creation and makes one feel like they are the very special apple of His eye.

Psalm 17:8 (KJV), "Keep me as the apple of the eye, hide me under the shadow of thy wings."

Jesus Christ is the master pastor-teacher, and we are the priceless pupils that He loves to spend time with and reveal His divine nature to in word and spirit.

Jesus said to me, "Follow Me, follow Me."

John 12:26 (KJV), "If any man serve me, let him follow me; and where I am, there shall also my servant be: if any man serve me, him will my Father honour."

My friend, the world is a dusty planet with rough and rugged places, yet we all call it our temporal dwelling place. But while we are living on Earth, we should be preparing our hearts for our spiritual departure some fine day.

Perhaps the spirit of religion would like to stone us for what we believe in Christ, but Christ is not confined to the restrictions of the nature of fallen man. Jesus is the master of all freedom, without confinements and sin.

Jesus Christ is the only man who ever breathed and walked upon the face of the earth that we should follow hard after with all our hearts and our living being so that we can walk all over heaven with Him one glorious day.

Here we are, friend, with the perfect choice to press hard after Christ in all His liberating expressions of holy truth that keep our hearts mindful of His celestial kingdom to the point that we outshine the noonday sun in the light of our salvation liberation. There is far more than we could ever dream or imagine that is available to us in our Christian walk with our Lord. He is a God of abundant overflow that is giving more than we ever could ask Him for. How simple it is to fully believe Him for spiritual things and how simple it is to abide in His holy freedom because Jesus Christ is our delivering master who goes before us and opens the way in illuminations of majestic glory light of heaven's sheer radiance in the sacred pages of His recorded truth in the earth.

May you embark on a journey today by looking up to heaven and wait upon the Lord to go before you in His all supreme authority and all-deserved glory, taking the word of life to the hearers and the hungry as many are destitute and waiting for the pure truth that can free them from the powers of darkness and sin's bitter enslavement.

Friend, your designed destiny is one of costly freedom and unlimited resources to finish your course and receive your crown of glory on heaven's celestial shore.

John 8:36 (KJV), "Therefore if the Son makes you free, you shall be free indeed."

My friend, you are free to be all that God alone has called you to be. Only believe. Have no doubt, for God has wonderful things in store for you. You are free to believe for greater and better things, according to the Word of God. You are free to rise in faith and believe with childlike faith for great and mighty things in the supernatural realm of God to manifest in your life here below. You are free to walk in the perfection of liberty and share your liberated life in Jesus Christ with the world.

You see, my friend, Christ's freedom is perfection as He alone is the perfect one, and He sets the captives free to freely express all of heaven's attributes on Earth.

There are so many missing truths that are not being taught in many pulpits today because of doubt, fear, and unbelief, and it is starving the souls of mankind of many joyous freedoms in Christ. May God have mercy! Amen.

Friend, we know that all the days are in our heavenly Father's hands, and He knows them from beginning to end, so you can deeply trust Him to order your steps right, and His kingdom best will richly shine through your anointed vessel. You can rest in His holy presence because He is going before you today with His fiery sword paving the way! Amen!

Following Christ to the End

The journey is long and filled with raging battles; Jesus has gone before you, reigning in all victory.

The valley is low; Jesus is walking with you in the lush green pastures arrayed with heaven's perfection and beauty.

The mountain is high; Jesus climbed it before you and is seated in the highest place of honor at the right hand of His Holy Father.

The cave is lonely and dark; Jesus is speaking the words of abundant life in His sweet fellowship with you.

The river is deep and wide; Jesus will not allow you to be swallowed up by the storms of life, for He will calm your

> heart to a serene stillness of deeper spiritual education.
>
> The wilderness is rugged and the desert barren; Jesus will give you living water and feed you fresh manna straight from the throne room of all-sustaining life and glorious fire.

Jesus Christ is the all-sustaining shepherd who wants to shepherd the heart all the way into His Father's eternal glory.

My friend, we need to always have the right attitude and mindset with the kingdom of God, clarity, and laser beam focus because our whole living being depends upon it.

As children of God, we need to identify our life in the salvation lifestyle of Jesus Christ, walking out our own identity and destiny in the Spirit of God!

We must daily seek to only live in the Word of God and rise in the full assurance of the resurrected life in Christ. One must stay fully convinced that God will do all that He alone has promised and that He will fulfill all as He faithfully safeguards the heart in these perilous times.

Remember, when we keep the right attitude toward God, we always soar at a high altitude in the Spirit of the very heart center of His kingdom identity.

Jesus loves to lead us and feed us with manna from above!

Complete Focus upon Jesus Christ

My friend, having our complete focus upon Jesus Christ and His supernatural kingdom keeps us in the living realities of expecting glory manifestations over and over again, whereby it is ever so pleasing to our heavenly Father as we just believe and richly receive His radiant kingdom lifeways.

When I was overtaken with the beauty of following Jesus with complete and uninterrupted focus, I knew all that was before me was my master and His royal kingdom. To me, that was total completion that needed no explanation but to only experience such divine guidance in a way that it was a celestial heaven on Earth. Friend, our primary focus should always be Christ and His kingdom; therefore, all else should be secondary.

Colossians 3:2 (KJV), "Set your affection on things above, not on things on the earth."

My heart was so full of the passion of heaven to stay in the mindset of being in the center of Christ's will and leaving all else at His anointed and powerful feet. I knew as I stepped onward after the shepherd of my soul that I would never lose focus of His presence and His Word governing my whole life. But we must always be mindful of this truth as this is a daily walk with the Lord. A laser beam focus on Jesus, the *Word*, is a powerful commitment with the reinforcement of Jesus Himself walking the straight and narrow path with each one of us, keeping us in the spirit of truth and wealthy revelations of supernatural fellowship. There is absolutely nothing in the whole universe that can provide such supernatural phenomena of wealthy experiences.

Friend, the Lord gave this word to me many years ago, and I speak it regularly. Many want the ways of the world and not the way of the *Word*. May we enter into the fulfilling focus of heaven today as it knows no distraction of the world at any turn. Our heavenly Father doesn't want us distracted by the ways of the world but only attracted and attentive to the holy ways of His covenant promises that bring heaven's best to a searching heart of complete surrender! We can't get anything better than that! Now, can we? Having heaven's best in our hearts today brings a glorious freedom that the devil cannot steal away.

My friend, you will always have the temptations of distractions to try and rob you of valuable focus and fellowship with your loving master, but you must be wise to these fleeting distractions of the world as they are always demanding your time and attention. It's a wise practice to have your focus on heaven above you, seeking God daily about how to wisely walk on the earth and live and occupy accordingly to His faithful words of wise instructions. I assure you, as a sold-out Christian, you will know when the enemy of your soul is placing a distraction before your face.

Matthew 6:33 (KJV), "But seek ye first the kingdom of God, and his righteousness; and all these things shall be added unto you."

Oh, what wonderful joy to gleam in as we put Jesus Christ and His kingdom first place in our hearts and lives.

Psalm 25:5 (KJV), "Lead me in thy truth, and teach me: for thou art the God of my salvation; on thee do I wait all the day."

God loves to lead us and feed us with His royal feast from His holy feasting place at the throne of eternal grace.

Smitten by the Sovereignty of Christ's Holy Freedom

My friend, what I mean by being smitten by the sovereignty of Christ's holy freedom was being strongly attracted to and captivated by the holiness of pure love in the spirit of righteousness, as this was the experience I had in the vision as I was following closely behind Jesus Christ my Lord. The greatest love that has ever stepped foot upon the planet Earth was and is our king, Jesus, who carried the love of His heavenly Father in His vessel and completely demonstrated the power of that highest love to all humanity.

I was aware of the heavenly freedom that was known by me and my master. It was an encounter where His presence was so tangible that His complete freedom was in glorious radiance to the point that I had such wisdom and knowledge of our divine intimacy of spirit to Spirit, mind to mind, and heart to heart with Him. My focus on Him was fixed and transfixed in the overwhelming feeling of a complete and real joy that was not generated by anything upon the planet Earth. I was walking in total freedom with my Lord, and my heart was harmonious with Him. His glorious love and presence went before me, preparing the way. In His holy leading, I was so happy to follow closely behind Him. I had a deep sense of trust that moved my heart to the blessed assurance that I was the Lord's and He was mine. I knew my master was so happy and pleased with me.

The beauty of the fascination of our freedom in Jesus Christ surpasses all documentation ever recorded in the highest form of governments that are established in the entire universe.

We have the freedom in Jesus our Lord to willfully bow down to His sovereignty and express the common goal of the strong unity of faith for our liberties in Jesus Christ as we stand in solidarity and harmony, so much so that we will never bow to the evil invasions of darkness that are threatening our very salvation lifestyle and that being a free moral agent of the king of glory! My friend, aren't you happy that God has a kingdom above that knows no end and that His dwelling place is holy and beyond all corruption, for His government is of eternal peace and everlasting love and *total truth* security?

This kind of celestial lifestyle awaits every born-again Christian who wholly follows the master. Friend, we must believe that there is a powerful lifestyle in Jesus Christ our Lord.

Let us look at these powerful scriptures in the Word of God.

> For unto us a child is born, unto us a son is given: and the government shall be upon his shoulder: and his name shall be called Wonderful, Counsellor, The mighty God, The everlasting Father, The Prince of Peace. Of the increase of his government and peace there shall be no end, upon the throne of David, and upon his kingdom, to order it, and to establish it with judgment and with justice from henceforth even forever. The zeal of the

Lord of hosts will perform this.

Isaiah 9:6–7 (KJV)

God rules over all nations, and His Son is the Savior of the world. At the throne of grace is the divine administration of God the heavenly Father, and at His right hand is our great governing king, Jesus, ruling in the holy authority of divine power. The kingdom of heaven is established in all truth and justice, weighing the hearts of man.

> All the ends of the world shall remember and turn unto the Lord: and all the kindreds of the nations shall worship before thee. For the kingdom is the Lord's: and he is the governor among the nations.
>
> Psalm 22:27–28 (KJV)

Proverbs 21:1–2 (KJV), "The King's heart is in the hand of the Lord, Like the rivers of water; He turns it wherever He wishes. Every way of a man is right in his own eyes, But the Lord weighs the hearts."

Friend, as we follow the ways of Jesus, our full attention is heavenward and filled with a joyous delight that showers rich blessings over our soul. For a child of God to be ruled by the God above and having Him lead in all royalty and righteousness is like the morning due, kissing the face of the earth, providing new life to all that benefit by His Holy Spirit outpouring fiery love touch.

Master of Royal Delight

My friend, back in the 1980s, I was enduring very hostile warfare, and while going through this unwelcome and perplexing war, the master spoke these beautiful words to me, "Will you always take delight in Me?"

I knew this was a very serious question that I had to ponder with diligent search before the throne of grace. In faith, I knew the rightful place of humility's unmerited favor, which is a sweet aroma before His face, Jesus Christ being the rose of Sharon, the royal delight of heaven given to us by God, our maker, of whom all supreme authority and the perfection of love belongs.

Oh, at the throne of grace, I learned early on in my Christian walk to stay before His face of sacred truth and to behold His glory, taking great delight in the holiness of His righteous redemption that burns powerfully with wisdom, making the reflection of heaven richly known to a sold-out heart of deep love for the Almighty God and His covenant promises.

In Him is all life, love, and complete freedom.

We see only You, Lord, and we desire none but Thee.

My friend, these comforting words in Zephaniah unfold the realization of the truth that our heavenly Father is 100 percent faithful to a believing heart because these promises are fireproof of His ageless and timeless truth that illuminates the heart with heaven's identity realities and destiny fulfillment. God's promises are true, holy true, and nothing but true, so let them flow through you, precious one. It's time to recognize His kingdom delight showering over you with the mightiness of His perfect love.

Zephaniah 3:17 (KJV), "The Lord thy God in the midst of thee is mighty; he will save, he will rejoice over thee with joy; he will rest in his love, he will joy over thee with singing."

My friend, His royal delight is our steadfast freedom fight for the holy truth on which the foundation of the world was framed. See Genesis 1–2.

Hebrews 11:3 (KJV), "By faith we understand that the worlds were framed by the word of God, so that the things which are seen were not made of things which are visible."

We were all created to worship God in His holy splendor and supernatural fame, declaring His great name and pure truth in the whole universe with delightful expressions of joy and explosive faith.

The master is the sweet shepherd of my soul, and oh, how I love Him so. For me to record these words from His heart to my heart for all of you to read and ponder such spirit life wonders of encouragement is a royal delight within my heart, as I know God takes pleasure in the hearts of His children that are fixed upon the His kingdom above and His wondrous Word that He gave us to richly live by here below. I truly pray that you run in the spirit life of supernatural freedom wonders and stand upon the Holy Word, believing that you, too, can embrace an abundant life in Jesus Christ to the point that all you desire is His pleasured treasures that are innumerable and never-ending.

Jesus is royal delight in the light of His Father's perfection in delivering truth and radiant love. He is the living hope of a more favorable life that brings complete happiness and everlasting joy to all who wholly serve Him. To know Him in the spirit of truth as He is truth, may we find our daily rest in complete delight as He is the eternal light that burns in all saved hearts the fiery desire to see His promised achievements of victory after victory.

My friend, let us live today in a much more wholesome and thankful way before the throne of grace, where we can abide in the Father's holy presence, having the sweet assurance of diligence to always be alert and delighting in heaven's royal attributes that are freely given to us by our heavenly Father, His Son Jesus Christ, and His precious Holy Spirit.

Friend, may we take this time and focus on taking delight in the creator in heaven and Earth as He alone is the Almighty God, and it's our treasured purpose within our earthen vessels to take great delight in our Holy God of intimate glory.

We need to focus daily on the sacred Scriptures and apply them to our humble hearts so we can live a life of holiness through the shed blood of Jesus Christ, our risen Lord. We must have a deep love for the Lord and His Holy Word, literally holding nothing back from Him as we know He already knows all things from the beginning to the end and nothing unknown in between. It is a fact that there is no lack in God. He loves to delight in His children! Only believe. He rewards faith!

Friend, when we walk humbly before God and speak of His Word without shame in this short-lived life, we are continuously celebrating the liberating force of delight in the grandeur of the God of the universe. God takes us seriously, and may we take Him seriously by serving Him with a whole heart willingly without reservation to the degree that all we see is our Heavenly Father daily beautifying us in His Son's Spirit-led and Spirit-fed lifestyle. Amen!

Psalm 149:4 (NKJV), "For the Lord takes pleasure in His people; He will beautify the humble with salvation."

God is pleased to call us His own, and He is pleased when we wholly follow Him home! Amen!

Friend, as I ponder today on the beautiful vision that I had following the master so many years ago, I richly celebrate the truth of knowing that the Word of God was walking so gently before me, and I wanted nothing before me but my glorious king and His kingdom. What a revelation to abide in constantly and that knowing Jesus Christ, the living and burning Word that burns with such deep love cascading over us, His glorious light, and life for all to partake of through His salvation experience. May we all take each day to look to the Lord for every single breath of life and the leading of it. We were created for His glory and His plan. That's not hard to comprehend, but it is so easy to believe. You see, my friend, the living reality of heaven is the very breath that you inhale and exhale; therefore, let it be settled today that you choose a more excellent way of living life looking up heavenward where God is sitting upon His royal throne.

In Genesis, God breathed life into the first man (Adam) that was ever created.

Genesis 2:7 (KJV), "And the Lord God formed man of the dust of the ground, and breathed into his nostrils the breath of life; and man became a living soul."

> O the breath of Life.
>
> God gave it all to the great and small.
>
> With each new breath, may we thank Him for the heartbeats that are given.
>
> His love created us, and His love looks daily upon us.
>
> With mercy and lovingkindness, our God sent His Holy Son to die for us so that we
>
> Could forever stay in His celestial kingdom, where death cannot enter.
>
> We shall forever partake of the bread of life in the royal feasting place at His holy throne of intimate grace.

Friend, what joy and liberty we have in God. I love to inhale His kingdom and exhale His love. Oh, His love divine and glory light sublime! Remember to take the time daily to ponder the holy wonders of God and His daily plan for your set-apart life.

It is so easy to follow the master! It truly is, so don't listen to the lies of hell and the lost world. Jesus Christ is the light of the world and the burning force of *truth* that brings wise and perfect guidance to all searching hearts.

John 8:12 (KJV), "Then spake Jesus again unto them, saying, I am the light of the world: he that followeth me shall not walk in darkness, but shall have the light of life."

When we follow Jesus Christ, we are following truth, as He is the walking sword of glory, wonders of His Father's heart, and His holy fire power. He is the eternal light of purity and all holiness and should daily be revered as the eternal heartbeat of His Holy Father.

Friend, one of the most powerful psalms in the Bible that David wrote is Psalm 119. It is a powerful resource that enlightens the heart to run swiftly to the infallible Word of God without delay and abide in the sacred Scriptures for daily life application and heart transformations. It is a beckoning call to the divine guidance of the heart of the Father unto His children, and in keeping His holy commands, one keeps the soul from the wicked contaminates of the fallen nature of man and the devil's invading deceptions.

I want to share with you some of the verses in Psalm 119. As you read through them, I pray you are engulfed with the heart of the heavenly Father and His loving joy as you partake of His divine nature of truth in the kingdom identity realities of His Spirit speaking to your spirit. His heart enflaming your heart with sweet fellowship of holy intimacy where your mind and whole vessel are flooded with the wisdom of an effervescent flow of heaven's holiness that cannot be quenched or diminished by any earthly woe.

> Blessed art thou, O Lord: teach me thy statutes. With my lips have I declared all the judgments of thy mouth. I have rejoiced in the way of thy testimonies, as much as in all riches. I will meditate in thy precepts, and have respect unto thy ways.
>
> Psalm 119:12–15 (KJV)

Psalm 119:49–50 (KJV), "Remember the word unto thy servant,

upon which thou hast caused me to hope. This is my comfort in my affliction: for thy word hath quickened me."

My friend, God's word is 100 percent true, and His truth will change your heart and life through and through. Following Christ is following truth! Amen.

John 14:6 (KJV), "Jesus saith unto him, I am the way, the truth, and the life: no man cometh unto the Father, but by me."

Jesus Christ Is the Truth

Truth will always do for you what nothing else on Earth can do.

Truth will keep you alive in the day of famine.

Truth will lead you in the presence of God and create within you an everlasting joy that is holy and preserved just for you!

Truth will reveal to you your designed identity in Jesus that is tried and true and solely ordained just for you and no one else!

Truth will always defeat the works of darkness before your face and cause you to enter into the rest of humility and kingdom identity covenant abilities.

Truth will guide you to the end with victorious validations of godly successes in pure authenticity.

Truth is all light and life within your saved heart that conquers all darkness, placing it all under your anointed feet forever to stay!

Truth will never lie to you but it will always expose all liars and wickedness plotting against your anointed life.

Truth will reveal to you more truth and promote you in the greater depths of righteous accelerations of wisdom and revelations.

Truth will keep your heart in perfect alignment with heaven's will for your daily life.

Truth will never lead you astray, for it will always lead you in all the right ways of the heavenly Father's desires concerning your daily existence on Earth.

Truth will establish you in the wealthy covenant plans of your heavenly Father so you can stand and feed upon the strength of His almighty power!

Truth will keep you in a conquering mode of covenant promises that are ageless and timeless without defeat and decrease!

Truth will quicken your heart to the ways of the Holy Father and cause you to shun the ways of the world.

Truth will cause you to be seated in heavenly places and increase the anointing upon your life!

Truth will keep your heart focused daily upon the perpetual illumination of the persistent call to wisdom and its eternal rewards.

Truth will reveal its dancing fire of spirit life within your saved heart of fiery faith.

Truth is God's perfect will for your life reflecting heaven's holy attributes to the lost world.

Friend, allow your tongue to be wise, speaking only truth and skilled in the Word of God because in following Christ, you will have great influence before fellow believers everywhere and the hearers of truth.

CHAPTER 5: HIS LIBERTY LIFE FORCE

Complete Freedom in the Holy Dance

My friend, back in the early 1980s, I had a glorious encounter with my king of glory.

I was spending time with the Lord throughout my day when the Holy Ghost spoke these beautiful words for me to go out onto the road in front of my home and dance before Him in worship. He was calling me into a higher realm of glorious worship, but when He first spoke to me to do so, I told Him that someone could drive down the road and so on…. Excuses are not accepted before the throne of God. I knew that this was a call straight from the throne room of God to obey and that I had to adhere to His beckoning call ASAP as God was seeking for me to come before Him that very moment. And so, I did just that.

This was my beautiful experience. As I began to gracefully dance before the Lord in a blissful dance, He began speaking to me, teaching about how powerful "dancing in worship" really is. He said, "When you dance before Me in worship, your whole vessel is in complete freedom before My throne. Heaven's freedom of expression is released within your surrendered and obedient heart to demonstrate it on the earth before all without reserve."

In my encounter, I was dancing in the all-consuming liberating power of the very fiery presence of the living God! It was as if I was raptured in the throne room presence at that moment! I felt such a supernatural strength and revival fire flowing through my yielded vessel that nothing of any evil force of hell or any human form on Earth could touch or stop my celebration of exuberant freedom and expression of divine worship before my heavenly Father. I was totally untouchable while worshipping God in the dance, and I was moving with a celebrated force of heaven. God was teaching me that dance is holy before His presence and how He loved to see His children dance before Him in complete surrender and beaming in fiery joy.

Dancing belongs to God, not the devil.

Dancing is glorious worship that is beautiful in the sight of God.

When this beautiful encounter happened to me, I had not seen dancing before the Lord in the traditional church that I attended while growing up. The Lord told me to teach people about worshipping Him in the dance, and I teach it unto this very day. It was something that had not been taught. I am a worshipper of dance unto the Lord as He will say to me these words in my alone time with Him as well, "Come before Me and worship Me in the dance, My daughter."

I am called into high praises where I am free to worship in my kingdom identity that is not of the world nor is it accepted by many in the church; however, we must only be God pleasers and obey Him to the fullest and never have the fear of man, which becomes a snare to the heart and enslaves the flesh!

Be free to dance today!

King David was a man after God's own heart and blazed with a wholehearted dance before the Lord, as it's recorded in the Bible. King David loved the presence of God, and he loved having the ark of the covenant in His presence. David's wife, Michal, despised him in her heart for his glorious dance in worship before his Holy God. David not only danced; he was shouting with all the house of Israel, along with trumpets blaring. What a holy and happy scene that must have been to behold. God loves to see us worship Him in spirit and in truth. What the church needs now are celebrations of high praises and worshipping in the dance.

Dancing before the throne is holy unto the Lord.

> And David danced before the Lord with all his might; and David was girded with a linen ephod. So David and all the house of Israel brought up the ark of the Lord with shouting, and with the sound of the trumpet. And as the ark of the Lord came into the city of David, Michal Saul's daughter looked through a window, and saw king David leaping and dancing before the Lord; and she despised him in her heart. And they brought in the ark of the Lord, and set it in his place, in the midst of the tabernacle that David had pitched for it: and David offered burnt offerings and peace offerings before the Lord.
>
> 2 Samuel 6:14–17 (KJV)

Friend, allow the Holy Spirit to take you into the joyous and harmonious heartbeat of the heavenly Father as you are fully synchronized with the Trinity in spirit and truth. Dancing in worship unto our Holy Father is an unspeakable and beautiful expression that displays heavenly attributes within your anointed vessel. The Lord spoke this to me in the '80s, "Allow Me to dance My fiery words across your heart."

Dance. Dance with all your heart unto your master, and be not ashamed to worship Him in your freedom expressions because He loves to watch you worship before His throne!

Friend, while you're in the fiery love chamber of His heart, allowing His Spirit life to dance across your heart, His manifested presence shows up powerfully in your life.

God loves to have His holy way within the heart and express Himself through it as He wills.

Psalm 30:11–12 (KJV),

> Thou hast turned for me my mourning into dancing: thou hast put off my sackcloth, and girded me with gladness; To the end that my glory may sing praise to thee, and not be silent. O Lord my God, I will give thanks unto thee for ever.

The scriptures in Psalms declare we go from mourning to dancing and removed sackcloth and girded us with gladness.

Friend, let us take our unashamed heart action and go before our king of glory with a jubilant force of celebration and rise in freedom release before our king!

Let us choose to dance.

Let us choose to shout.

Let us choose to sing.

Let us choose to lift up holy hands.

Let us choose to bow low and kiss the feet of our master.

Oh, let us choose wisely without hesitation before the throne of grace.

Let us choose to give God all the glory and be unashamed to demonstrate our willful adoration to the creator of the universe.

Friend. It's dangerous to be ashamed of God and His kingdom's ways in the earth.

Luke 9:26 (KJV), "For whosoever shall be ashamed of me and of my words, of him shall the Son of man be ashamed, when he shall come in his own glory, and in his Father's, and of the holy angels."

I encourage you to never be ashamed of Jesus Christ and His salvation lifestyle that transforms our lives as Christians into His very likeness of the high quality of living life in His Father's holy attributes.

Romans 1:16 (KJV), "For I am not ashamed of the gospel of Christ: for it is the power of God unto salvation to every one that believeth; to the Jew first, and also to the Greek."

God is so glorious, and He has left His perfect words to instruct us; therefore, let us make His praise glorious without reserve and restrictions. The world and the spirit of religion do not want Christians to celebrate our joyous life in Jesus Christ by praising powerfully, shouting victoriously, and dancing freely. They don't want us to live our destiny identity in the authority and anointing of Jesus Christ.

One must wisely choose to live life being led by Jesus Christ, the foundation of truth in all supreme authority and authenticity.

> Praise ye the Lord. Praise God in his sanctuary: praise him in the firmament of his power. Praise him for his mighty acts: praise him according to his excellent greatness. Praise him with the sound of the trumpet: praise him with the psaltery and harp. Praise him with the timbrel and dance: praise him with stringed instruments and organs. Praise him upon the loud cymbals: praise him upon the high sounding cymbals. Let every thing that hath breath praise the Lord. Praise ye the Lord.
>
> Psalm 150:1–6 (KJV)

The Fiery Kiss of His Presence

Song of Solomon 1:2 (KJV), "Let him kiss me with the kisses of his mouth: for thy love is better than wine."

The fiery kiss of His presence loves to envelop a humble and searching heart in the intimate holy place of His captivating fellowship embrace! The divine kiss of the master is the Word of truth that permeates all of heaven and all of Earth! The blazing force of the kiss of truth is like a flaming torch that can never be put out, and its nature is the burning realization of a great and mighty champion who is unconquerable at every turn, our triumphant Messiah Himself!

In my throne room encounter, every word that the Father spoke to me was a mighty blazing force of elegance and unity in the same mindset of complete agreement (fully in sync), which is eternal. His kiss of truth is a seal of covenant knowledge in the Spirit of the Holy Father, Jesus Christ, His Son, and the comforter, the Holy Spirit! Friend, just the radiance of His presence causes one to be in a place of wholehearted surrender and willful obedience! The only thing you can do in the throne room presence of love is relentlessly submit to the flaming torch and love touch of heaven's ministry desires for your life! Plain and simple! Jesus Christ, the living Word of God, kissed the earth with His holy presence one fine day, and the whole world has not been the same since the day of His covenant birth.

There are scriptures in the Bible that state to greet one another with a holy kiss. It is recorded in the Strong's Concordance that the Greek definition of a holy kiss is "to love," and the usage is: I love (of friendship), regard with affection, cherish; I kiss.

John 3:16 (KJV), "For God so loved the world, that he gave his only begotten Son, that whosoever believeth in him should not perish, but have everlasting life."

In this powerful verse of Scripture, we see the kiss of God's perfect love manifesting powerfully in His Word (Jesus Christ) as He became the ultimate sacrifice on Calvary's cross and lived out His kingdom identity on Earth.

Many in modern-day churches do not practice greeting one another with a holy kiss. When you ponder the Scripture references about a holy kiss, it's evident that we have gotten away from the holy practices of the early church and the written Word on many powerful things that God designed for us to daily put into practice.

In Strong's Greek definition, a holy kiss is a kiss to show respect or affection between friends.

His holy kiss is a kiss of all eternal truth. As salvation's acceptance, the spiritual kiss of divine holiness builds the glorious salvation foundation of truth and justice, riding out in victorious might as Jesus is all light. His kiss is a holy kiss of royalty and majestic power, which is Jesus Christ, the eternal kiss of life.

"All the brethren greet you. Greet ye one another with an holy kiss" (1 Corinthians 16:20, KJV).

"Greet all the brethren with an holy kiss" (1 Thessalonians 5:26, KJV).

"Greet one another with an holy kiss" (2 Corinthians 13:12, KJV).

"Greet ye one another with a kiss of charity. Peace be with you all that are in Christ Jesus. Amen" (1 Peter 5:14, KJV).

Friend, our heavenly Father has great love and holy affection for all humanity, and He longs to daily kiss our hearts with His words of life so that we can live a more abundant quality of life that the world cannot offer or create because it can only be achieved through the salvation kiss of Jesus Christ our loving Savior.

Friend, the greatest kiss of life is the salvation kiss of Jesus Christ's love fire. The greatest affection on Earth that you will ever encounter is the love of God in Jesus Christ, His Son! Oh, let His love fire burn and save you from the powers of the wicked deceptions of hell. The lies of Satan are deceptive darkness that separates a soul from the rich spiritual life of intimacy with the Holy Father. Don't fall trapped in the works of evil because of following the carnal ways of man and the deceptions of the spirit of religion.

The Flaming Torch of His Liberty Life Force

Come alive in the jubilant force of heaven today and show the world your mighty, victorious stance in Jesus Christ, your king of glory!

God desires for us to be a flaming torch of His liberty life force, taking His kingdom identity realities to the nations of the earth.

Jesus Christ is the glory torch of the Holy Father's love that makes us one perpetual flame, that being the bride of Christ blazing in the holy fire of His all-consuming end-time-revival attire, transforming hearts around the globe.

The heavenly Father wants the redeemed of the Lord flaming powerfully in the shining glory of their anointed Savior.

> For Zion's sake will I not hold my peace, and for Jerusalem's sake I will not rest, until the righteousness thereof go forth as brightness, and the salvation thereof as a lamp that burneth. And the Gentiles shall see thy righteousness, and all kings thy glory: and thou shalt be called by a new name, which the mouth of the Lord shall name. Thou shalt also be a crown of glory in the hand of the Lord, and a royal diadem in the hand of thy God. Thou shalt no more be termed Forsaken; neither shall thy land any more be termed Desolate: but thou shalt be called Hephzibah, and thy land Beulah: for the Lord delighteth in thee, and thy land shall be married. For as a young man marrieth a virgin, so shall thy sons marry thee: and as the bridegroom rejoiceth over the bride, so shall thy God rejoice over thee. I have set watchmen upon thy walls, O Jerusalem, which shall never hold their peace day nor night: ye that make mention of the Lord, keep not silence, And give him no rest, till he establish, and till he make Jerusalem a praise in the earth. The Lord hath sworn by his right hand, and

by the arm of his strength, Surely I will no more give thy corn to be meat for thine enemies; and the sons of the stranger shall not drink thy wine, for the which thou hast laboured: But they that have gathered it shall eat it, and praise the Lord; and they that have brought it together shall drink it in the courts of my holiness. Go through, go through the gates; prepare ye the way of the people; cast up, cast up the highway; gather out the stones; lift up a standard for the people. Behold, the Lord hath proclaimed unto the end of the world, Say ye to the daughter of Zion, Behold, thy salvation cometh; behold, his reward is with him, and his work before him. And they shall call them, The holy people, The redeemed of the Lord: and thou shalt be called, Sought out, A city not forsaken.

Isaiah 62:1–12 (KJV)

Our salvation is here in the life of Jesus Christ and His obedience to willfully die upon a wooden cross. Jesus Christ is the flaming torch of His liberty life force that is burning pure righteousness with all intercessions at the right hand of God.

Jesus Christ will not remain silent as His presence is our liberty life force, and He will not remain silent until we come forth as His end-time flaming torch of radiant truth. When His covenant word penetrates the atmosphere in all authority, principalities disappear from our presence, fleeing in terror without refuge, but they are only cast back to hell where they originally came from.

The king of glory is strong and mighty and mighty in battle.

The same Jesus that walked the earth over 2000 years ago is walking the earth today by His Holy Spirit, drawing hearts to His salvation, beckoning call for total surrender and complete servanthood. He is raising up an army of believers who will not bow down to Lucifer and all the demons that were cast out of heaven with him.

> And there was war in heaven: Michael and his angels fought against the dragon; and the dragon fought and his angels, And prevailed not; neither was their place found any more in heaven. And the great dragon was cast out, that old serpent, called the Devil, and Satan, which deceiveth the whole world: he was cast out into the earth, and his angels were cast out with him.
>
> Revelation 12:7–9 (KJV)

Friend, isn't it wonderful to read the Holy Scriptures of God and hear of these profound happenings as God revealed scriptures unto mankind?

The devil can never live in heaven again. He is eternally defeated!

> How art thou fallen from heaven, O Lucifer, son of the morning! how art thou cut down to the ground, which didst weaken the nations! For thou hast said in thine heart, I will ascend into heaven, I will exalt my throne above the stars of God: I will sit also upon the mount of the congregation, in the sides of the north: I will ascend above the heights of the clouds; I will be like the most High. Yet thou shalt be brought down to hell, to the sides of the pit. They that see thee shall narrowly look upon thee, and consider thee, saying, Is this the man that made the earth to tremble, that did shake kingdoms.
>
> Isaiah 14:12–16 (KJV)

CHAPTER 6: HIS SUPERNATURAL IDENTITY MANIFESTING IN OUR TIME

You Were Created for God's Divine Purpose

Friend, I live my life seeking the face of God and His Word. I embrace the supernatural reality of God's kingdom in total child-like faith, believing that God can do anything at any time and anywhere He wants to, as He will always do as He pleases. He is God all by Himself, and it's best that all mankind learn that His supernatural nature loves to demonstrate in this natural world, and nobody has the power to control God and the wise presence that longs to make Himself known to us however He desires!

Friend, in all my beautiful encounters with the master, I love the realization that I completely have the heart action of *faith* and no *doubt* in believing that God is a Spirit and He wants to deeply communicate with me on many levels; therefore, I was never bound by the spirit of religion in thinking that I had to have any person's permission to believe God and to know Him in His freedom expressions of all truth and supernatural demonstrations in my life and the lives of others.

Be informed that the devil hates that God manifests His supernatural ways on the earth; that is why he has deceived many with unbelief, doubt, fear, and lack of knowledge.

I pray these words encourage you to the highest as you must *only believe* that you were created by God to experience great and mighty things on the earth through the salvation word lifestyle of Jesus Christ and His divine Holy Spirit of illumination and holy demonstrations.

God created all for His glory, and He loves to reveal to you supernatural things with the perfect balance on the just scale of spirit and truth so you can walk in the divine order of heaven.

Ephesians 2:10 (KJV), "For we are his workmanship, created in Christ Jesus unto good works, which God hath before ordained that we should walk in them."

You are a free moral agent of the king of glory, and you are free to be all that He alone has called you to be!

Friend, be a servant unto righteousness, having your heart melted in holiness and daily right standing with God.

> Being then made free from sin, ye became the servants of righteousness. I speak after the manner of men because of the infirmity of your flesh: for as ye have yielded your members servants to uncleanness and to iniquity unto iniquity; even so now yield your members servants to righteousness unto holiness. For when ye were the servants of sin, ye were free from righteousness. What fruit had ye then in those things whereof ye are now ashamed? for the end of those things is death. But now being made free from sin, and become servants to God, ye have your fruit unto holiness, and the end everlasting life. For the wages of sin is death; but the gift of God is eternal life through Jesus Christ our Lord.
>
> Romans 6:18–23 (KJV)

You can freely embrace the supernatural nature of God, the heavenly Father, Jesus Christ the Son, and the comforter, the Holy Spirit.

Friend, when you freely embrace His supernatural nature, you will flourish in the deeper things of His Holy Spirit where you are only satisfied with more of His Word and glorious Spirit in all liberation accelerations!

> If ye love me, keep my commandments. And I will pray the Father, and he shall give you another Comforter, that he may abide with you for ever; Even the Spirit of truth; whom the world cannot receive, because it seeth him not, neither knoweth him: but ye know him; for he dwelleth with you, and shall be in you.
>
> John 14:15–17 (KJV)

Resist the Lying Spirit of Religion

Friend, it's time to come up higher in the Spirit of God and His liberty force of increase in wisdom, knowledge, and understanding and be totally set free from the carnal captivity of the spirit of religion that is a killing and thieving force of hell. Resist the temptations of the spirit of religion because it always wants one to follow man's rules and regulations, forming the controlling enslavement of ritualism in the heart, leaving it with a death cycle of grave deceptions.

Matthew 23:27 (KJV), "Woe unto you, scribes and Pharisees, hypocrites! for ye are like unto whited sepulchres, which indeed appear beautiful outward, but are within full of dead men's bones, and of all uncleanness."

The spirit of religion can never say what or who you are in God. God Himself will tell you who you are and teach you to walk in the feeding and leading of the Holy Spirit's power and authority.

The spirit of religion always has a disorderly habitation. In Jesus Christ's freedom, there is nothing but a holy habitation for the heavenly Father's ever-abiding presence.

Jesus Christ Seated upon His Throne

I love this supernatural encounter that Isaiah experienced as he saw in a vision the Lord sitting upon His throne high and lifted up! His encounter with the Lord is of a majestic force that took the prophet into a burning place of a holy mandate and mission to get the kingdom of God's work accomplished with great power and commitment. I love the profound and impacting words of Isaiah in Isaiah 6:8 (KJV), "Also I heard the voice of the Lord, saying, Whom shall I send, and who will go for us? Then said I, Here am I; send me."

Friend, what powerful words came after one of the seraphim touched Isaiah's lips with the burning life coal from the altar that altered the rest of his life. His iniquity was removed, and his sins were purged. He was ready and released by God and sent out to the people as a powerful prophet in his day, ministering as the very fire of God's holy mouth. The beauty of the prophet Isaiah is that he lived a holy life solemnly in the reverential fear of God. He also lived a continual life of obedience before God.

Friend, when I had my open vision of Jesus sitting upon His throne, He later took me to Isaiah 6 and asked me if I would go to the peoples of the earth.

I said, "I will go; send me."

Little did I know then that He was going to call me in February of 1990 to a major airline so I could travel the world, taking the gospel and His love to souls everywhere that I traveled.

> In the year that king Uzziah died I saw also the Lord sitting upon a throne, high and lifted up, and his train filled the temple. Above it stood the seraphims: each one had six wings; with twain he covered his face, and with twain he covered his feet, and with twain he did fly. And one cried unto another, and said, Holy, holy, holy, is the Lord of hosts: the whole earth is full of his glory. And the posts of the door moved at the voice of him that cried, and the house was filled with smoke. Then said I, Woe is me! for I am undone; because I am a man of unclean lips, and I dwell in the midst of a people of unclean lips: for mine eyes have seen the King, the Lord of hosts. Then flew one of the seraphims unto me, having a live coal in his hand, which he had taken with the tongs from off the altar: And he laid it upon my mouth, and said, Lo, this hath touched thy lips; and thine iniquity is taken away, and thy sin purged. Also I heard the voice of the Lord, saying, Whom shall I send, and who will go for us? Then said I, Here am I; send me. And he said, Go, and tell this people, Hear ye indeed, but understand not; and see ye indeed, but perceive not. Make the heart of this people fat, and make their ears heavy, and shut their eyes; lest they see with their eyes, and hear with their ears, and understand with their heart, and convert, and be healed.
>
> Isaiah 6:1–10 (KJV)

The Lord spoke these words to me many years ago while working a flight and descending for arrival into Detroit, Michigan, as I was looking down at the lights at night in the Detroit landscape, "If My people realized that the supernatural realm was more real than the natural realm, they would never be the same again." Jesus Christ's divine nature is a revealing nature that places one in the heartbeat of heaven so that we can receive more spiritual life on

Earth.

We need to allow the light of truth (Jesus Christ) to reveal more truth to our hearts as the days unfold in our quest and diligent search for more of His kingdom identity realities.

Friend, I want to share with you my open vision of Jesus Christ sitting upon His holy throne in the early 1980s. He swiftly appeared before me in such power and glorious dominion as I was standing in my kitchen where I once lived in Bronson, Michigan. I could not make out any of His facial features, as the whole vision was a beautiful outline of His fiery presence of eternal glory. The whole vision was a glory light of liquid fire moving; it was so brilliant as likened unto the beauty of a pearl but far more distinctive than that of the beauty of a pearl in the natural world. It was so profound that words cannot explain or fully compute the experience of this vision. I was so in awe of the liquid fire (light) burning, but it was not that of the fire we see in the natural world. I remember it as clearly today as if it was just yesterday; that is how vivid it still is within my mind and etched deeply within my heart.

Jesus Christ had many crowns stacked upon His head. In this glorious vision, I knew that Jesus was giving me a command that would carry me on throughout the rest of my life.

He was seated on a throne that was huge and wide. The outline was a perfect cut in the vision. Jesus Christ took His right hand and raised it before me to a certain height. His robe had wide flared sleeves, and the right one dropped a certain degree. As He lifted His right arm, He began to speak Isaiah 41:10 to me.

Isaiah 41:10 (KJV), "Fear thou not; for I am with thee: be not dismayed; for I am thy God: I will strengthen thee; yea, I will help thee; yea, I will uphold thee with the right hand of my righteousness."

Friend, the piercing sword of the Lord that penetrates the heart burns a realization that the shepherd's voice is the only voice that matters, and the ears are fine-tuned to the triune God as the heart is set ablaze with covenant promises that are forever burning in holy glory before the throne of God. Jesus speaks Spirit to spirit.

I was totally in the Holy Ghost with my master as He spoke powerfully with great authority and security. He is so powerful, so majestic, and so glorious in His kingdom identity and holy authenticity! All I could do was just be so transfixed by His glorious presence as it was swift and powerful, and it left me with a deep desire to hunger and thirst for more of His kingdom lifestyle. I knew it would require a high price and a very lonely life for me to experience the rest of my days. I must say now that I am in my sixties, I've lived a life longing for the heart of my heavenly Father. It's worth it all! It's worth all the sacrifices and the high cost that I have truly had to pay.

When Jesus Christ speaks to you, it's like time stops and stands still and nothing at all matters but His fiery presence and holy truth and radiant glory that is before your face. You realize you are so undone as He is perfectly holy and sinless!

Repentance is more than a thought; it becomes a heart action of a swift bowing in low estate of humility before His presence, and the heart is melted like wax.

John 16:13 (KJV), "Howbeit when he, the Spirit of truth, is come, he will guide you into all truth: for he shall not speak of himself; but whatsoever he shall hear, that shall he speak: and he will shew you things to come."

I AM That I AM

I AM that I AM is in Jesus Christ, who is in us as born-again children of God, our supernatural kingdom identity in the natural realm.

I AM that I AM lives within us!

God wants to live (*big*) in our hearts in these final hours, but we must become as He is in the life of His written Word (Jesus Christ, our covenant truth).

Jesus said that we are one with Him and His heavenly Father. Therefore, let us live, breathe, and teach His identity destiny in the heart of His Father! Amen! See John 17:21–23.

Friend, on the night of Jesus' betrayal, a band of officers came seeking to take Him captive, and Jesus spoke to them in John 18:6, saying, "I am he," and they fell backward to the ground. What power and authority from His heavenly Father (I AM that I AM) that demonstrated through Jesus Christ, His Son. That same power is available to us through Jesus Christ, our Lord and Savior.

The power of God is alive in our day, and He performs many miracles, signs, and wonders. God's power never died out with the last disciple as He is moving powerfully and demonstrating miraculously as He did in their ordained days upon the earth.

> And Judas also, which betrayed him, knew the place: for Jesus ofttimes resorted thither with his disciples. Judas then, having received a band of men and officers from the chief priests and Pharisees, cometh thither with lanterns and torches and weapons. Jesus therefore, knowing all things that should come upon him, went forth, and said unto them, Whom seek ye? They answered him, Jesus of Nazareth. Jesus saith unto them, I am he. And Judas also, which betrayed him, stood with them. As soon then as he had said unto them, I am he, they went backward, and fell to the ground.
>
> John 18:2–6 (KJV)

The supernatural power is in the earth as God is in the earth, performing His Word and will.

Friend, be mindful daily of the presence of God and His voice that wants to guide you in ways that you have not yet stepped into. Still, you must allow Jesus to rule your life so you experience the kingdom identity realities that are His wise teachings and supernatural experiences.

Speak, Lord. Speak…

We are listening.

We are waiting.

We are trusting.

We are expecting.

We are believing.

We are free to obey Your Word.

We speak boldly Your sacred Word to hearts here below; we speak with authority, knowing You receive all the glory, honor, and praise!

We love receiving Your instructions because we know in keeping your commands there is a great reward in the end.

With every word that You speak, Lord, there are accelerations of kingdom-manifested life!

Your spoken Word brings an increase to the human spirit that causes a release of love that pours into the heart the living hope and sustaining grace.

Your spoken authority melts our hearts with Your anointed commands, demolishing strongholds and causing our hearts to tremble and quickly obey.

You are our teacher and the keeper of our hearts, revealing truth to every inward part of our created hearts.

Oh, shepherd of our soul, we love hearing Your sacred voice and reading Your Holy Word because You keep us alive in the day of famine by feeding us the feast from Your throne room of eternal life and power!

When Jesus appeared before me in this open vision, I was so thrilled beyond comprehension that I was engulfed in His presence, so much so that I knew His presence was all that mattered! He was first and foremost the king of glory, and He wanted first place in my heart and life!

I knew His command of *truth*, as all His commands are not to be taken lightly but literally, as His Word will always burn greater spiritual life in the seriousness of His kingdom identity and profoundly develop His authentic identity within our surrendered hearts.

Matthew 6:33 (KJV), "But seek ye first the kingdom of God, and his righteousness; and all these things shall be added unto you."

Friend, we must always put Jesus Christ and His kingdom lifeways before our dreams, lands, egos, and plans! Amen!

Put Your First Love First

Jesus, You desire to be our first love, as You have a godly jealousy that is holy, pure, and true! Reigning over us Your majestic glory from above, You require us to seek You first with no idols in sight! You want us to seek Your face and to know Your heart. We love communing with You before Your mercy seat.

Your holy fire transforms our humble vessel. We love to burn in Your glory fire of revelation illuminations!

You love to set us free on a humble and bent knee before Your throne of grace.

You require of us total surrender and holiness.

You love for us to seek You early, awaiting Your perfect guidance in spirit and in truth.

You love to show us Your mighty acts as we fully believe without the plagues of doubt, fear, and unbelief.

You love to build and thrill us with the holy governing foundation of truth that makes a perfect plumb line straight to the throne of grace.

You love having first place in our hearts so that You can perform Your glorious wonders freely without any restraints.

You love it when we freely believe all Your promises with child-like faith and great anticipation.

You love to speak to us in any way You please!

You love it when we love You and worship You just because You are the great I AM that I AM, and You faithfully kiss our hearts with Your Son's forgiving love!

You are Almighty God, omnipotent, immortal, invisible, and are from everlasting to everlasting! We love You, king of glory!

We richly celebrate our victorious life that is fully captivating in You!

Friend, it is so simple to believe that God wants to visit Your life in a profound way. First, you must believe that He is a rewarder of those who seek Him.

Hebrews 11:6 (KJV), "But without faith it is impossible to please him: for he that cometh to God must believe that he is, and that he is a rewarder of them that diligently seek him."

Friend, you must also cast off all the ways of doubt, fear, and unbelief and rise in bold faith and secure belief because the spirit of religion and hell never want a heart after God to discover the freedom in the Word of God and His intimate fellowship that is available to all believers around the whole world. Amen.

> For verily I say unto you, That whosoever shall say unto this mountain, Be thou removed, and be thou cast into

> the sea; and shall not doubt in his heart, but shall believe that those things which he saith shall come to pass; he shall have whatsoever he saith.
>
> Mark 11:23 (KJV)

Friend, doubt, fear, and unbelief are enemies of the heart.

Jesus appeared to His disciples in John chapter 20, but Thomas was filled with doubt.

> Then saith he to Thomas, Reach hither thy finger, and behold my hands; and reach hither thy hand, and thrust it into my side: and be not faithless, but believing. And Thomas answered and said unto him, My Lord and my God. Jesus saith unto him, Thomas, because thou hast seen me, thou hast believed: blessed are they that have not seen, and yet have believed.
>
> John 20:27–29 (KJV)

Friend, it is imperative to trust and believe. As Jesus said to Thomas in verse 29, "Blessed are they that have not seen, and yet have believed."

Jesus is not walking on the earth in the flesh as He did on the day of His disciples, as recorded in John chapter 20, but by His Spirit. He is with us, and He wants us to believe and embrace the supernatural spiritual life.

Thomas started out with doubt and ended up in the tangible manifested truth before His face, for then was He satisfied. But Jesus wanted Thomas to have the heart action of the other disciples, and that meant they only believed. You must choose every day that you have life upon this temporal earth to reach beyond yourself and touch the heart of God with your child-like faith and welcome Him to have His perfect and supernatural way to manifest and demonstrate heaven in your midst! Amen.

Remember, God wants to commune with us, but we must live in holiness before His throne, making it a daily practice as best we can. We humans do fall short, so we must swiftly repent of our rotten flesh mess of darkened sins.

The Lord spoke these words to me years ago: Repentance means to turn away from, not run back to the old sinful ways. We cannot be foolish and turn back to the old ways of the flesh.

Proverbs 26:11–12 (KJV), "As a dog returneth to his vomit, so a fool returneth to his folly. Seest thou a man wise in his own conceit? there is more hope of a fool than of him."

Examine your heart and ask God to burn out everything that's not of Him.

Friend, we must be swift to repent and serve God with our whole hearts until our last day upon the earth. We must have clean hands and a pure heart before the Lord. Amen!

Embrace the supernatural abundant life in Jesus Christ by letting go of all that holds the heart down in the natural realm of sinful nature. Let us look at some sinful traits that may hold one in bondage to the works of the flesh:

Lying.

Doubt.

Fear.

Unbelief.

False doctrine.

Pride.

Arrogance.

Stubbornness.

Deceptions.

Hard heart.

Bound by religion.

Traditions.

Ways of God seem foolish to you.

Lack of knowledge.

Refuse to read the Word of God and apply it.

Refuse to have a deep prayer life.

Refuse to listen to the voice of the master.

Refuse to obey the voice of the master.

Quenching the Holy Spirit.

Grieving the Holy Spirit.

Ashamed of the Holy Spirit.

Open rebellion.

Scoffing and mocking the Scriptures.

Resisting the Holy Ghost.

Gossiping.

Limiting God.

Living in hypocrisy.

Love the ways of the world.

Refusing salvation.

Witchcraft practices.

Refusing to sell out to God.

Having a form of godliness but denying the power.

Lust of the flesh.

Idolatry.

Envy.

Jealousy.

Fits of anger.

Drunkenness.

Sexual immorality.

Rivalries.

Divisions.

Dissension.

Heart filled with hate for another person.

Unforgiveness.

Covetousness.

Spiritual identity theft.

Malice.

Love of money.

Addictions.

Blasphemy against the Holy Ghost.

Friend, you don't want anything in your heart that robs you of a closer walk with the heavenly Father, Jesus Christ, His Son, and the glorious Holy Spirit.

You always want your heart right with God in order to live in the wealthy depths of the bridegroom chamber of His holy heart and His supernatural manifestations.

CHAPTER 7: WELCOME TO THE SUFFERING SIDE OF CHRIST

Rejection Is Always Before Our Lord

Luke 17:25 (KJV), "But first He must suffer many things and be rejected by this generation."

Jesus Christ was rejected all the way to the cross, yet He was gloriously resurrected into the eternal kingdom of perfection acceptance before God, His heavenly Father. Amen!

Friend, Jesus Christ is the divine perfection of heaven, and many on Earth could never accept Him or the divine power He walked in. He is still rejected by many today.

God spoke this word to me many years ago, "Have you been falsely accused, wrongfully judged, and horribly misunderstood? Welcome to the suffering side of Christ!"

It is so true. Isn't it?

When you have been falsely accused, wrongfully judged, and horribly misunderstood, you are completely being rejected.

There have been people in my life who did not understand the anointing that I walk in, nor do they want to, and that's okay. I'm so used to these types of behaviors in my midst. It's all good as my life is all for God's glory and harvesting of souls. I live to please God, not man or woman.

Our wonderful king of glory was mistreated as well, but far more so than what we will ever experience.

Friend, do you feel like everywhere you turn, rejection is slivering around you and wanting to strike its venomous flame at you?

Rejection, rejection, rejection.

Rejection here.

Rejection there.

Rejection everywhere.

Rejection was the life of Jesus Christ.

Rejection is suffering for Christ's sake.

Rejection is the work of hell.

Rejection produced tears in my eyes, but God bottled them up in heaven.

Rejection calls you evil; God calls you chosen and redeemed.

Rejection strikes its jealous flames; God enflames your humble heart with holy acceptance.

Rejection is a working of hell that has to lick the dust under your anointed feet.

Rejection has no power over your saved and accepted heart before the throne of grace.

Rejection is darkness that cannot penetrate the light of truth that guards your heart.

Rejection of God is Satan's eternal damnation curse. Jesus redeemed us from the curse.

Friend, there will always be rejection and persecution against the Lord's anointed ones.

Luke 10:16 (NLT), "Then he said to the disciples, 'Anyone who accepts your message is also accepting me. And anyone who rejects you is rejecting me. And anyone who rejects me is rejecting God, who sent me.'"

Friend, I must share this true gospel news with you today. As you are alive on Earth, there will always be a daily reality of being rejected by some people. Be still, take a deep breath, and rest in the sweet assurance of heaven that illuminates your path with the blissful knowledge that our rejected Lord will never leave you in the heartache of rejection. Remember, you are accepted and deeply loved before the throne of grace!

There are many wounds that invade our lives, but there is a healthy spiritual remedy that Jesus provided when He became the redeemer for all of mankind. So, today, if you are experiencing an open wound of rejection or another wound, open the Word and apply its righteous instructions for the betterment of a healthy heart and a happier state of living in heaven's ever-abiding peace. Amen! Be healed today in Jesus Christ's name!

Friend, Jesus Christ is all power and all authority over all the forces of evil. God is always wooing our hearts to go deeper into His Word and Spirit with Him as He is the most knowledgeable teacher that ever walked upon the earth.

When rejection invades your life, rebuke it in Jesus' name and enjoy the short-lived test that is in your life. A swift promotion comes with a greater increase and release of His anointing when one endures trials and tests of all kinds.

There is such a fiery depth of pure love in the life of Jesus when you know that you are living in the tangible rejection as our master did when He walked the earth in the flesh form of a man. It makes one stop and think and follow hard after the ways of the gospel of Jesus. Oh, what joy and rejoicing that holds true in the shining heart of every believer saved by the glorious, redeeming power of Jesus Christ's radiant lifestyle.

Friend, when the enemy is working to kill you, God is healing your heart in multiple ways! The abundant life of Jesus Christ and His power of deliverance will keep you burning in the fire of His perfect performance of grace upon grace and anointing upon anointing. Oh! What sweet fulfillment belongs to you! Take it! Take it now In Jesus' holy name and His glorious unashamed fame!

Like the woman with the issue of blood, I had spiritual warfare issues of rejection in all directions.

She touched the hem of His garment and deeply moved His heart, so much so that the healing virtue went out of His holy body and healed her suffering body and changed her life before the multitudes!

> And a woman having an issue of blood twelve years, which had spent all her living upon physicians, neither could be healed of any, Came behind him, and touched the border of his garment: and immediately her issue of blood stanched. And Jesus said, Who touched me? When all denied, Peter and they that were with him said, Master, the multitude throng thee and press thee, and sayest thou, Who touched me? And Jesus said, Somebody hath touched me: for I perceive that virtue is gone out of me. And when the woman saw that she was not hid, she came trembling, and falling down before him, she declared unto him before all the people for what cause she had touched him, and how she was healed immediately. And he said unto her, Daughter, be of good comfort: thy faith hath made thee whole; go in peace.
>
> Luke 8:43–48 (KJV)

The Lord spoke this word to me for many years in Luke 8:48.

I have always told the Lord that I was a woman of great faith, and

He would say back to me, "It takes great faith to have great faith." God is forever our great faith. Amen!

For all the decades of rejection that I have experienced, I have also loved all of the glorious education that God has deposited within my heart, and it has been rewarding to serve the Lord with all my heart as I daily enter His presence with the living faith and abundant joy of saying it is well—it is well.

The Lord has richly taught me how to go from healing to housing His words of perfection deeply within my heart so that my vessel is always in a preserved place of a higher state of living, which is the highest place, the throne room of intimate grace.

My heart was completely healed of all the horrid rejection that I suffered during this unwanted battle that was waged against the anointed one that lives in me! His name is Jesus Christ, the anointed one! Press through all the carnal mess in this world with a driven force of heaven's holiness, and you will enjoy living in all of heaven's kingdom identity victories!

The Beauty of Rejection

The beauty of rejection is having His holy reflection shining brightly within our hearts! Amen!

The enduring love of Jesus has fully accepted me.

The mercy of God has gently covered me.

The hope of heaven floods my heart with kingdom expectancy.

The joy of heaven strengthens my pure heart for greater assignments.

The peace of heaven shields my kingdom identity purpose.

The glory of God overtakes my spirit with greater wisdom.

The Word of God requires more of my undivided attention.

The presence of God welcomes me with His open arms and open heart of wealthy treasures.

The beauty of His holiness is my sacred lot, and hell's onslaughts cannot steal it away!

The Holy Spirit is my paraclete, who will never leave my side, for He is our constant guide to righteous living! Amen.

The authority of heaven is forever settled in my heart.

The suffering silence of Jesus Christ opened the way for my victorious voice of holy boldness!

The beauty of rejection has allowed my heart to become a vessel of honor before my heavenly Father.

Oh yes, suffering is worth it all and completely understood by Jesus, our king!

He is the perfect reflection of the sufferings we endure in the fallen world. Amen.

Be encouraged, friend. Just as I press on in my walk, you can, too! Only believe!

Let your heart sing a new song!

Let the wisdom of God rule your heart through all the onslaughts you face.

Oh, what glorious wonders of heaven that freely flow through an accepted vessel, one that is full of humility and a deep thirst for the greater glory realm of the kingdom of God.

Be Wise and Stay Free in Your Anointed Destiny Identity

Jesus Christ daily lived knowing that He was rejected. He was never moved by the carnal ways of fallen man who rejected Him or anything else on Earth that went against His heavenly Father's holy ways. All workings of hell never defeated His anointed walk or work that the heavenly Father destined Him to fulfill. Jesus Christ never came to Earth for Himself; He came to the earth for all of us and for us to freely invite His saving power into our hearts.

The true light is Jesus Christ, and as He moved in the glory of His Father, He did so with the mission of demonstrating His royal kingdom to all mankind. There was nothing that could take His freedom in the power of His priestly anointing. May we strive to be as Jesus Christ in the way that He dealt with multiple situations of fallen man and woman and the powers of Satan.

> That was the true Light, which lighteth every man that cometh into the world. He was in the world, and the world was made by him, and the world knew him not. He came unto his own, and his own received him not.
>
> John 1:9–11 (KJV)

Jesus went to His own, and they did not receive Him, but other people did, and they received the glorious things of His holy kingdom and loved to hear of the teachings of His Father's kingdom and His holy angels. To believe and receive Jesus' presence was amazingly powerful, as we see the glorious benefits to those who had their experiences with Jesus recorded in the Holy Bible.

Friend, as you are raised up with Jesus Christ in heavenly places, you will richly draw out more kingdom reflections of His nature and shine forth in the holy attributes of His power. Note: Ephesians 2:6. Therefore, you will never be moved by the carnality of man or the attacks of hell as you are one with Christ Jesus, and that is all that matters, for all else will fall in place as you stay before His face and keep ministering to hearts as God commands. He will richly commend you for doing so! Amen.

Ephesians 2:6 (KJV), "And hath raised us up together, and made us sit together in heavenly places in Christ Jesus."

Friend, I was created to go to people around the globe and share the gospel with hearts, so whether people receive my anointing or not, it's okay because God is always looking for and rewarding a humble heart that is tried and true and one that seeks to live in obedience.

The opinions of others don't move me; only the covenant commands of God burn powerfully within me.

The more excellent weight of glory is for us to behold and embrace in the fiery heart of God, where the life of our vessel is purified and refined in the fire of His holy desires. Oh, the sweet test of afflictions do we pass and rejoice in the blissful education transformations from glory to glory, seeing the eternal destination richly before us! Press on. Press on in Jesus' name! Press on. Press on in His eternal and rewarding flame and holy fame!

> For our light affliction, which is but for a moment, worketh for us a far more exceeding and eternal weight of glory; While we look not at the things which are seen, but at the things which are not seen: for the things which are seen are temporal; but the things which are not seen are eternal.
>
> 2 Corinthians 4:17–18 (KJV)

Soaring above Rejection

We keep our eyes looking upon our resurrected Lord, and we soar in the fiery kiss of acceptance before His holy throne of grace. Keep the thoughts of rejection under your feet and give no place to its toxic ways that want to distract you from your kingdom focus and mandate mission! Amen!

God takes great pleasure in our heart action of forgiveness!

It is the will of God for us to forgive those that do us wrong. We cast it all at the feet of Jesus. Oh yes, we do.

God will deal with all hearts as He always has and always will. There are thousands upon thousands of written commands revealed in the Holy Bible, reminding us how to live in the divine order of heaven so we can secure our eternal home. Amen.

Friend, when we abide in His presence daily and live our lives seeking the rich manna of heaven through the unfolding of the living Word of God and applying its recorded pages to our saved lives, we are then fully surrendering our sold-out and set-apart vessels to the perfect plan of our loving Father and Jesus Christ, His Son, through the power of the Holy Spirit.

Remember, the way to soar above rejection is by staying in His holy love fire of complete forgiveness, where the heart greatly abides in the anointed liberation of constant increase before the throne of grace. Rejection is always present in the world, but it has no power over the (Word) Jesus Christ within the heart of a born-again believer.

Agape Love Is Our Destiny Identity in Christ

Love is grand, and loving others is a written command from the Lord.

Agape love is unconditional love, and it melts the heart with the eternal flame of heaven's revelation. Agape love is deeper than any sin and more powerful than anything on Earth. Unconditional love is the heart of the heavenly Father, for He will always love humanity; that's true, but in order to spend eternity with Him, we all must live according to the sacred Scriptures and become born again through Jesus Christ. Amen.

Friend, let the agape love of heaven be a mighty flowing fountain hitting all who step into its surging flow, keeping the humble heart aglow with the resources of truth that light the path more into the excellence of Jesus Christ's nature.

Love covers a multitude of sins.

"And above all things have fervent charity among yourselves: for charity shall cover the multitude of sins" (1 Peter 4:8, KJV).

"For I reckon that the sufferings of this present time are not worthy to be compared with the glory which shall be revealed in us" (Romans 8:18, KJV).

Learn to rejoice in warfare, for out of your deep sufferings will be the birthing of a great ministry, reaping heaven's soul harvesting and holy rewards!

The ministry depths of agape love are glorious indeed, so start stepping out in the celebrations of accelerations where promotions in the anointing are limitless and constantly burning more of the majestic ways of the heart of God within your spirit so you can richly enjoy being more than a conqueror in heaven's rewarding strength.

John 15:18 (KJV), "If the world hate you, ye know that it hated me before it hated you."

Friend, what an honor it is for me to experience being rejected as Christ was because just as the world hates Him, so it hates us, and I say to that, "We are in good and holy company." Amen.

The more that people went against me, the more the Lord called me into His holy bridegroom chamber of fiery truth. He taught me profoundly how to obtain the mind of Jesus Christ and His Spirit-led attributes that safeguarded my heart from being swayed to the left or the right in every invading attack here below because I knew full well without waver that the high and Holy God over the universe was teaching me mightily how to walk in and exercise His everlasting dominion with love leading the way. All hell and everything else was out of my way, being ashes under my feet!

God is faithful to protect us, teach us, and go before us, destroying all works of darkness! Amen!

Friend, there are times in my life when I ponder how all alone on this earth I really am. I always call upon my master as He alone fully understands the powerful anointing that I carry in my vessel. He was the one who placed this anointing upon my life, and I'm thankful that He did, as it is helping souls. Many will never understand what it's like for a woman in ministry doing the works of the Lord because that alone takes rejection and persecution to a whole new level. I must say!

The Lord spoke these powerful words to me decades ago, and I joyously carry them deep in my heart, "You are never alone because you are never without the Almighty!"

Jesus Christ is in my heart to stay, and nothing outside of His truth can ever pull me away. The more I'm hated by hell and humans alike, the more I am determined to take His flaming sword of truth to a lost and dying world without regret. I will not bow to a devil, nor the fear of man nor the carnal ways of the rotten flesh mess that wars against the Spirit of our master. All hell is under my feet, and all of heaven's blessings and provisions are with me.

I know that many of you reading this today can relate to the written words and experiences in this chapter.

Don't give up; keep looking up and praising His holy name and glorious fame because God has you all wrapped up in His agape love. He also has you demonstrating heaven's persistence with His shining glory shining brighter than the noonday sun.

Psalm 37:6 (NLT), "He will make your innocence radiate like the dawn, and the justice of your cause will shine like the noonday sun."

Sure-Footed upon His Heights

"He will keep the feet of his saints, and the wicked shall be silent in darkness; for by strength shall no man prevail" (1 Samuel 2:9, KJV).

Friend, the ways of the world are slippery and rugged with darkness and defeat, but the way of the master is a straight path of victory and living life in the highest place at the feet of Jesus before the throne of grace. Although there are so many serious battles against our lives, just know this one thing: God is leading you to His eternal heights with purified faith, moving in the constant momentum of perfect love and the glory flames of rewarding endurance. Rejoice, rejoice, for the battle has been won. Let the joy bells of heaven ring loudly within your heart as you stay focused on the master leading you into His hideout of perfect strength.

Friend, let the heights of His glory abide in your enduring vessel and awaken you to the fullness of Christ.

Stay focused on the fullness of Christ and not the rejection of man, for your spiritual well-being totally depends upon the Word of God and His salvation deliverance plan. God wants you walking and living freely in the anointing that He placed upon you. Remain sure-footed with the Word of God being your guide, and you will faithfully stand where angels stand.

> Yet I will rejoice in the Lord, I will joy in the God of my salvation. The Lord God is my strength, and he will make my feet like hinds' feet, and he will make me to walk upon mine high places. To the chief singer on my stringed instruments.
>
> Habakkuk 3:18–19 (KJV)

"He maketh my feet like hinds' feet, and setteth me upon my high places" (Psalm 18:33, KJV).

"God is my strength and power: and he maketh my way perfect. He maketh my feet like hinds' feet: and setteth me upon my high places" (2 Samuel 22:33–34, KJV).

Friend, a hind is a female deer that is a sure-footed animal; she has the capability to place her hind feet in the exact same place where her front feet were as to be climbing on cliffs and on dangerous terrain. She can climb up to high places in total safety as God created her hind legs to maneuver to achieve her high place of strong standing without falling or failing in her climb.

Sure-footed in Greek means "without stumbling or falling."

Jesus Christ is not a stumbling block but the chief cornerstone that the builders rejected, and upon His foundation of truth, you can be encouraged by this in His full acceptance at the throne of grace, more grace will be given for you to rise higher in your Christian walk of kingdom fame. Praise His holy name, mighty warrior! Keep marching! Keep climbing! Keep rising and shining!

Get to dancing upon the heights in Jesus' name!

You Are Not an Outcast

Friend, many years ago, I told the Lord that I felt like such an outcast, and these words came swiftly within my heart, "You are not an outcast, and you will never be cast out of My presence."

What a glorious word from my king of glory, and I say to you today, "You are not an outcast when Jesus is the Savior of your soul." Oh no, you are a burning flame shining in His glory fire life, listening to His saving voice of profound wisdom. Oh, how He loves you and how He died to save you and indwell within your heart.

We are saved to go to the outcast bringing heaven's words of life to them. We are free daily to move forward, taking the gospel and healing power to all people, great and small.

> Even unto them will I give in mine house and within my walls a place and a name better than of sons and of daughters: I will give them an everlasting name, that

shall not be cut off. Also the sons of the stranger, that join themselves to the Lord, to serve him, and to love the name of the Lord, to be his servants, every one that keepeth the sabbath from polluting it, and taketh hold of my covenant; Even them will I bring to my holy mountain, and make them joyful in my house of prayer: their burnt offerings and their sacrifices shall be accepted upon mine altar; for mine house shall be called an house of prayer for all people. The Lord God, which gathereth the outcasts of Israel saith, Yet will I gather others to him, beside those that are gathered unto him.

Isaiah 56:5–8 (KJV)

What beautiful words to the prophet Isaiah, but these words apply to us in our day as well as we are adopted into Jesus Christ. Note: See Ephesians 1:5.

God is the reigning power of salvation to all, and the freedom force in Jesus Christ has brought us into the divine freedom of heaven so that we remain steadfast and unmovable through the power of Christ that rests upon us. Friend, it is so beautiful to experience the nature of Jesus Christ, for it is through His divine nature that we act wisely and carry His victory banner high in the natural realm. Our spirits are in the holy flow of kingdom identity realities, and we gracefully, in all humility, move in a Spirit-led motion of constant advancements. We are never moved by anything on the earth or under the earth that does not line up with the truth! We are always moved by the Word of God, our risen king, and His Holy Spirit.

Here we are in His holy mountain, holy presence, and holy throne room! We give Him praise, and we make our petitions known before Him and pray and forgive all who have wronged us throughout our lives. We repent and ask for forgiveness for hurting others as well. In Jesus' name!

God Hath Shined

I want to share with you an open vision that I had in a hotel room many years ago. There was a bright light that came into my room; it began to get larger and brighter, moving with a swift motion toward me with such brightness. The Lord has shown me his glory rain, which is what I call it, since the early 1980s. Friend, I want to encourage you to use your child-like faith and believe in God to show you things in the supernatural.

Friend, in our daily walk with the Lord, we can be in the shining place of His forever reigning glory as the light of Jesus Christ gave us access into the heart of God in His highest place, where we are untouched by the carnal ruinous of the world.

> The mighty God, even the Lord, hath spoken, and called the earth from the rising of the sun unto the going down thereof. Out of Zion, the perfection of beauty, God hath shined. Our God shall come, and shall not keep silence: a fire shall devour before him, and it shall be very tempestuous round about him. He shall call to the heavens from above, and to the earth, that he may judge his people. Gather my saints together unto me; those that have made a covenant with me by sacrifice. And the heavens shall declare his righteousness: for God is judge himself. Selah.
>
> Psalm 50:1–6 (KJV)

The devouring fire of God goes before Him. His fire is shining upon your life, and it's high time to step into your favored place before the throne because you have allowed God to be the all-consuming holy nature of your heart and complete vessel. Note: Psalm 97:3; Proverbs 11:27.

What shining beauty from God's Holy Spirit and pure truth from above shines favor and wise maturity in our hearts each new day because we choose to stay above all the carnal distractions.

Friend, we live in our identity in Jesus Christ; therefore, rejection and being an outcast are cast down and cast off and completely away from our presence in Jesus' name! Amen!

You have favor with God and full acceptance before His throne!

It's time to send up high praises to the heavenly Father! March on!

CHAPTER 8: KNOWING JESUS AS A LAMB TO THE SLAUGHTER

He Opened Not His Mouth

Friend, when Jesus opened not His mouth even in the silent suffering, He knew that He was in His Father's perfect will, fulfilling the prophets' scriptures as recorded in Isaiah 53.

What beauty we see in this timeless chapter of sacred truths as Isaiah is prophesying the future death of the promised Messiah.

> Who hath believed our report? and to whom is the arm of the Lord revealed? For he shall grow up before him as a tender plant, and as a root out of a dry ground: he hath no form nor comeliness; and when we shall see him, there is no beauty that we should desire him. He is despised and rejected of men; a man of sorrows, and acquainted with grief: and we hid as it were our faces from him; he was despised, and we esteemed him not. Surely he hath borne our griefs, and carried our sorrows: yet we did esteem him stricken, smitten of God, and afflicted. But he was wounded for our transgressions, he was bruised for our iniquities: the chastisement of our peace was upon him; and with his stripes we are healed. All we like sheep have gone astray; we have turned every one to

his own way; and the Lord hath laid on him the iniquity of us all. He was oppressed, and he was afflicted, yet he opened not his mouth: he is brought as a lamb to the slaughter, and as a sheep before her shearers is dumb, so he openeth not his mouth. He was taken from prison and from judgment: and who shall declare his generation? for he was cut off out of the land of the living: for the transgression of my people was he stricken. And he made his grave with the wicked, and with the rich in his death; because he had done no violence, neither was any deceit in his mouth. Yet it pleased the Lord to bruise him; he hath put him to grief: when thou shalt make his soul an offering for sin, he shall see his seed, he shall prolong his days, and the pleasure of the Lord shall prosper in his hand. He shall see of the travail of his soul, and shall be satisfied: by his knowledge shall my righteous servant justify many; for he shall bear their iniquities. Therefore will I divide him a portion with the great, and he shall divide the spoil with the strong; because he hath poured out his soul unto death: and he was numbered with the transgressors; and he bare the sin of many, and made intercession for the transgressors.

Isaiah 53:1–12 (KJV)

Friend, when Jesus Christ was being falsely accused by the chief priest and elders, He literally answered not a word to them. His silent suffering spoke innumerable volumes of pure truth and power to the invisible realm and to the visible state of affairs because Jesus Christ's obedience to His heavenly Father was the living, breathing prophecy of all time that God had intended for His holy fulfillment of higher kingdom plans that the world and Satan could not fully analyze or nullify. Jesus Christ's obedient steps to the cross ushered Him into His awaited eternal authoritative position at the right hand of power. Lucifer and all devils and all human enemies could not get in the way of heaven's fulfillment of Jesus Christ's eternal destiny, and nothing can keep you from your inherited destiny identity in Christ and His eternal home on high! Amen.

Hebrews 12:2 (KJV), "Looking unto Jesus the author and finisher of our faith; who for the joy that was set before him endured the cross, despising the shame, and is set down at the right hand of the throne of God."

Luke 22:69 (KJV), "Hereafter shall the Son of man sit on the right hand of the power of God."

Jesus Christ's kingdom identity is the one and only sacrificial lamb that would take away the sins of the world. Jesus redeemed us from the curse of the law as He became a curse for us.

> And when he was accused of the chief priests and elders, he answered nothing. Then said Pilate unto him, Hearest thou not how many things they witness against thee? And he answered him to never a word; insomuch that the governor marvelled greatly.
>
> Matthew 27:12–14 (KJV)

Jesus Christ remaining silent before Pilate was the act of His Holy Father's supreme authority encompassing all the covenant promises of prophecies that were God-breathed and that being that Jesus alone knew the beauty that was set before Him and the new covenant lifestyle that would be given to all born again believers as a holy inheritance that was not created or purchased by any sinful nature of humanity. The ways of man are futile. Note: Psalm 94:11 (NKJV), "The Lord knows the thoughts of man, that they are futile."

> When the chief priests therefore and officers saw him, they cried out, saying, Crucify him, crucify him. Pilate saith unto them, Take ye him, and crucify him: for I find no fault in him. The Jews answered him, We have a law, and by our law he ought to die, because he made himself the Son of God. When Pilate therefore heard that saying, he was the more afraid; And went again into the judgment hall, and saith unto Jesus, Whence art thou? But Jesus gave him no answer. Then saith Pilate unto him, Speakest thou not unto me? knowest thou not that I have power to crucify thee, and have power to release thee? Jesus answered, Thou couldest have no power at all against me, except it were given thee from above: therefore he that delivered me unto thee hath the greater sin. And from thenceforth Pilate sought to release him: but the Jews cried out, saying, If thou let this man go, thou art not Caesar's friend: whosoever maketh himself a king speaketh against Caesar.
>
> John 19:6–12 (KJV)

Friend, we do not like suffering, but as we read in Isaiah 53:7, the prophet Isaiah states two times how Jesus Christ opened not His mouth as He would be led to the old rugged cross where He would hang by three nails and die a horrid and agonizing death as the sin of all humanity was placed upon His sinless body, for He had to become the living sacrifice offered up to God, His heavenly Father. We love to know and experience such freedom in the life of Jesus our Lord, having access to the throne of grace through Jesus Christ's redemption offered on the Cross. However, we should not take His death and His persecutions for granted. We need to look at His obedience to the cross as an opportunity to live in the holy presence of God daily and live out a victorious destiny in the divine nature of Jesus Christ Himself.

While Jesus Christ was before Pilate, He marveled greatly. Jesus

Christ was the greatest living and breathing prophecy that was promised to mankind, as He is the living Word of God. We see in John 19:10 where Pilate speaks to Jesus Christ, saying that he had power over him to crucify him; however, the Lord knew His plan to be the sacrificial lamb before the world, and He went forth in ultimate humility to His death, burial, and resurrection. Therefore, Jesus did answer Pilate with His kingdom authority, telling him he had no power at all against Him, except it be given to him from above. Let us ponder the wonders of our glorious Messiah as He stood before men in the Holy Scriptures, demonstrating to them how He lived and breathed the Spirit of His Holy Father in all love, power, and authority, leaving people marveling and speechless to the many manifested wonders of His perfect kingdom identity reality in His Father above.

Matthew 28:18 (KJV), "And Jesus came and spake unto them, saying, All power is given unto me in heaven and in earth."

We Esteemed Him Not

Isaiah 53:3 (KJV), "He is despised and rejected of men; a man of sorrows, and acquainted with grief: and we hid as it were our faces from him; he was despised, and we esteemed him not."

Friend, Jesus Christ was not respected by some as He should have been while walking on the fallen and dusty planet. Our holy master was so despised by many that they turned their faces away from Him, but in His rich love and mercy, His face looked upon all mankind with holy compassion and pure forgiveness.

Friend, do you sometimes feel despised by many around you?

You are in good company! Jesus Christ walked that long before you. Remember, keep your heart fixed upon Christ and release all at His holy feet, then walk on in faith, hope, and love with the Lord being by your side. Amen! March on, friend! March on!

There were many times in this life when I received no respect from certain people, especially as a woman minister chosen by God to take the gospel to the world in word and powerful demonstrations of the Holy Ghost's power. I live my life before the throne, and that is my great joy; therefore, I don't need the praises of any flesh.

I know many of you out there are very disrespected because of the gospel of Jesus Christ and the ministry that God has ordained for you. Well, rest assured; God is working a far greater honorable plan for you before His holy throne, and that is far better than anything in this world. We don't seek the accolades of the ways of the world and the flatterings of mankind. That carnal mindset is crushed under our anointed feet! Amen!

Remember to keep your heart guarded from the multiple forms of temptations.

The Lord spoke this word to me when I was going through a series of spiritual warfare attacks; it has ministered greatly to my heart, "Many do not respect you or the anointed that I have placed upon your life. But I respect you." God is most glorious!

It's only in Jesus Christ alone! I boast the most in the Holy Ghost! He gets all the glory. See 2 Corinthians 10:17.

God alone sees all that you do for the gospel's sake, and that is truly all that matters, as we do not live our lives to be seen of flesh or to seek their praises.

God alone gets all the glory and all the praise, and that is thrilling and fulfilling to my heart as I live my days on the earth to please Him and serve Him to the fullest.

Friend, I know God is pleased with a heart that is working to help equip every born-again believer for the advancing of His kingdom through wise biblical teachings that empower the heart to rise in its God-given destiny and step out in the world using rich discernment that will safeguard the heart and mind from the hostile invasions of the seducing spirits and doctrines of demons that have targeted every born-again believer in today's world. Friend, we have much to get accomplished for the kingdom of God, as a quick work of heaven is operating in today's day and age.

God loves to use you for His glory and make His mighty power known to the people on Earth.

As a Lamb to the Slaughter

Friend, in Isaiah 53, we read that He was brought as a lamb to the slaughter. The wickedness that was constantly plotting against our Lord was that of a demonic origin.

Jesus Christ had many enemies who hated Him with such cruel hatred. We read how the scribes and Pharisees were so driven by the evil ways of Satan to the point that they became so consumed with the killing force that they had to see Him being led as a lamb to the slaughter.

Psalm 44:22 (KJV), "Yea, for thy sake are we killed all the day long; we are counted as sheep for the slaughter."

Friend, do you feel like you are counted as sheep to the slaughter?

In my own personal life, I have experienced this life from the time of my salvation in 1980. I'm sure for some of you, it's your walk as well.

When we are born-again Christians full of the Holy Ghost's power, we are a threat to hell and the works of the spirit of religion. But Jesus Christ, our Lord, is our defending defense of truth that forever stands. Amen!

We must serve Jesus Christ faithfully to the end and rejoice knowing we are His faithful witnesses, and we shall live with Him one fine day in His holy kingdom of forever peace and harmony!

Luke 22:2 (KJV), "And the chief priests and scribes sought how they might kill him; for they feared the people."

Jesus was performing miracles from God, His Father, and because of the good kingdom identity works that He was doing, the more hell wanted Him taken out of the world. What cruel jealousy and envy possessed the cold hearts of the religious scribes and Pharisees.

Friend, Jesus performed many miracles before the multitudes of people, and many loved Him and longed to follow His righteous ways. They were hungry for His profound and impacting teachings. What a glorious sight it must have been seeing Jesus Christ walking the earth in the flesh and showing the world His great compassion and deep love for souls.

> Then saith he to the man, Stretch forth thine hand. And he stretched it forth; and it was restored whole, like as the other. Then the Pharisees went out, and held a council against him, how they might destroy him. But when Jesus knew it, he withdrew himself from thence: and great multitudes followed him, and he healed them all; And charged them that they should not make him known: That it might be fulfilled which was spoken by Esaias the prophet, saying, Behold my servant, whom I have chosen; my beloved, in whom my soul is well pleased: I will put my spirit upon him, and he shall shew judgment to the Gentiles.
>
> Matthew 12:13–18 (KJV)

As a lamb to slaughter,

He was led.

In pleasing His Father, He opened not His mouth.

He was despised and rejected by many,

Yet, many loved Him deeply.

Thirty-nine stripes ripped deeply into His back,

His stripes brought us healing.

What a glorious benefit to receive healing.

Although the hatred was vile, He freely obeyed His Father.

He longs to fellowship with us.

He was afflicted, smitten of God,

He endured the cross for all the lost.

He is the rock of our salvation.

He became sin for us,

Who knew no sin.

Wearing a crown of thorns upon His head.

He was the perfection of humility!

Nails pierced His hands and feet.

Oh, how beautiful are His feet that spread the gospel.

He was given vinegar to drink.

He is the living water.

A spear pierced His side,

Killing brought forth His resurrection life.

His kingdom identity is our covenant reality.

He gave us all a choice to freely choose His glorious kingdom life or refuse His beckoning call. Choose Jesus. In choosing Jesus, you choose eternal life without end.

His love bled, and His love hung upon the cross of Calvary for all humanity alike so that we could live in the divine destiny of His supernatural kingdom identity realities in holiness and agape love.

"For he hath made him to be sin for us, who knew no sin; that we might be made the righteousness of God in him" (2 Corinthians 5:21, KJV).

Jesus Christ moved with the deep compassion of His Father's heart, and the tender love touched the multitudes, making new believers as He was sent from town to town. He is an incomparable, unconquerable, and indescribable king of glory who just wanted mankind to be redeemed from their sins and live in the divine nature of heaven's holy attributes! Amen!

Living a Sacrificed Life before the Throne

Proverbs 14:12 (KJV), "There is a way which seemeth right unto a man, but the end thereof are the ways of death."

Friend, we must strive to live a life consecrated unto God as best as we can. We must daily die to our old rotten flesh mess of the carnal nature.

I want to share with you an encounter I had many years ago in the presence of God while I was seeking his face.

Suddenly, God revealed to me how terrible the old flesh really is; it wants to war against the spirit. I was obeying God and doing as I should as a Christian and servant of His kingdom; however, He wanted to reveal to me that our flesh is that of an enemy nature against the spiritual ways of heaven; it must be daily consumed in the fire of His presence. So, let us look at some scriptures that apply to this subject that will set your searching heart in the full motion of wise applications of God's fiery truth and leave the heart yearning for more holiness and less attention, settling in the ways of the world instead of being consumed with the spiritual knowledge and understanding that subdues the lust of the flesh and the pride of life placing them always under our anointed feet!

For the flesh lusteth against the Spirit, and the Spirit against the flesh: and these are contrary the one to the other: so that ye cannot do the things that ye would. But if ye be led of the Spirit, ye are not under the law. Now the works of the flesh are manifest, which are these; Adultery, fornication, uncleanness, lasciviousness, Idolatry, witchcraft, hatred, variance, emulations, wrath, strife, seditions, heresies, Envyings, murders, drunkenness, revellings, and such like: of the which I tell you before, as I have also told you in time past, that they which do such things shall not inherit the kingdom of God. But the fruit of the Spirit is love, joy, peace, longsuffering, gentleness, goodness, faith, Meekness, temperance: against such there is no law. And they that are Christ's have crucified the flesh with the affections and lusts. If we live in the Spirit, let us also walk in the Spirit. Let us not be desirous of vain glory, provoking one another, envying one another.

Galatians 5:17–26 (KJV)

Friend, we must allow Jesus Christ to rule our hearts, removing daily all the fleshly desires that try to invade our lives. God wants all of us to live in the Spirit and hide the word deep within our hearts.

We need to daily resist the devil and his temptations that come before us.

Spiritual warfare is very hostile and intense in our day, and here are some spiritual warfare strategies to help you overcome the evil one.

James 4:7 (KJV), "Submit yourselves therefore to God. Resist the devil, and he will flee from you."

Submit in Greek means "to abide, surrender."

Resist in Greek means "to take a firm stand against."

Fiend, when you know evil is present, command it to flee. When the tempter comes to attack, open your mouth and declare this, "The blood of Jesus defeated you, devil. I command you to flee in the name of Jesus." This is taking authority over the devil in spoken word declaration. In Genesis, God spoke the world into existence. So, you can speak the devil out of your life. Amen!

Jesus spoke to the devil. See Luke 4.

Speak with authority in your salvation lifestyle. You have the authority through the shed blood of Jesus upon Calvary!

Friend, we defeat demons by the Word of God and the blood of Jesus. Amen.

Don't say, "Devil, please leave!" No! Instead, rebuke the devil out of your life. Say these words, "I command you to flee in Jesus' name! Amen."

There are many in the modern-day church that do not teach people how to take authority over the devil at all. God have mercy.

This is a very serious time, and it is imperative for born-again believers to resist hell and welcome heaven to have its most holy way within their lives every day.

A sacrificed life will keep your heart in right standing with God, growing up in the Word and Spirit, moving forth in greater maturity and security of your identity destiny, with kingdom clarity being your keen discernment.

Revelation 12:11 (KJV), "And they overcame him by the blood of the Lamb, and by the word of their testimony; and they loved not their lives unto the death."

We must die daily to the old flesh, placing all its desires under our feet, and seek God daily and His guidance for our righteous living accountability.

> I beseech you therefore, brethren, by the mercies of God, that ye present your bodies a living sacrifice, holy, acceptable unto God, which is your reasonable service. And be not conformed to this world: but be ye transformed by the renewing of your mind, that ye may prove what is that good, and acceptable, and perfect, will of God.
>
> Romans 12:1–2 (KJV)

Friend, you must present your body as a living sacrifice, as it is acceptable to God.

We must have a transformed mind through the Holy Word of God.

The Lord spoke this to me years ago, "You must have a Word-filled mind, Spirit-filled mind taking on the mind of Christ." We do that by reading the Holy Bible and applying it to our daily lives as it transforms our thoughts, our hearts, and our actions.

We must daily lay all at His feet in complete surrender. Give God all that you are and all that you aren't; He is the God of all glory, honor, and praise. Amen. He specializes in changing hearts and lives.

Friend, do you truly want the heart of God more than anything in the whole world? Remember, it's a daily choice to go the way of the Word or the way of the world.

Joshua 24:15 (KJV),

> And if it seem evil unto you to serve the Lord, choose you this day whom ye will serve; whether the gods which your fathers served that were on the other side of the flood, or the gods of the Amorites, in whose land

ye dwell: but as for me and my house, we will serve the Lord.

Choose wisely the way of the master and live a holy life before the throne, for without holiness, no man shall see the Lord.

Hebrews 12:14 (KJV), "Follow peace with all men, and holiness, without which no man shall see the Lord."

Friend, you can live a very victorious life in the presence of God and abstain from the works of the flesh and the pride of life. Every day, make it a practice.

Our heavenly Father wants His way, His will, and His Word to be the center of our hearts and lives every day in the spirit of holiness and righteousness.

When God deeply consumes your heart with truth, and you have deep convictions, you will instantaneously know that you have been transformed into the likeness of your creator over that of the creature. That, my friend, is a glorious revelation demonstration. Amen.

Many will not receive the transformation in your life but you must ask yourself this question: Do I want all that God Has for me? It will be worth it all! All the mistreatments and everything else that you endure. Just remember, Jesus endured the cross with joy! You will always be mistreated by many, but you can endure hardships for the cause of Jesus Christ as a lamb to slaughter because all His torturous moments are the reaping of monumental freedoms that you richly experience day by day.

A Prophetic Word

Come forth, my child, in your destiny identity that I designed for you in My deity.

My heart is the burning force of all supernatural life and life in the universe.

Within My heart, you humbly exist, partaking of the divine wealth of My kingdom bliss.

Look at the heavenly wonders above, knowing that you outshine My created galaxies.

Stand in awe and rest in peace and speak with all kingdom authority and secure boldness.

Fear no flesh as you keep marching forward in your quest, living out the words of My written Word until I receive you unto Myself in My holy kingdom.

Deceit Was Never in His Mouth

Friend, Jesus Christ never had a lie roll off His tongue; only love and truth ruled His heart and life because His flaming sword of truth cut down all the lies of the devil and also that of humanity, consuming them with His heavenly Father's fiery love of righteous accountability and holy justice. Truth is always justice and righteous judgment that keeps one's spiritual life in complete tact in these days of Word famine and great adversity.

When we live in truth and speak truth, we grow up powerfully in our destiny identity before the throne of grace only to display the living proof of heaven's sacred truths in our hearts and visible actions before all.

Numbers 23:19 (KJV), "God is not a man, that he should lie; neither the son of man, that he should repent: hath he said, and shall he not do it? or hath he spoken, and shall he not make it good?"

God is a God of truth, all truth and all holy *truth* in one man, the man Jesus Christ. As God revealed His perfect Son of love and truth to usward, we must strive to live before His throne in all truth and abstain from the ways of lies!

Friend, one sure way to inherit the kingdom of God is to live in pure truth and speak it constantly out of the mouth; telling the truth is easy, but telling a lie is a hard path of self-destruction, causing one to reap a bitter end of utter distrust. The devil is the great deceiver, and he is always slivering around to gravely deceive a heart. The Word of God will keep your heart clean with words that bring conviction and transformation.

A lie defiles the heart. What comes up out of your heart and rolls off the tongue reveals what is really in the heart and spirit.

Matthew 15:11 (KJV), "Not that which goeth into the mouth defileth a man; but that which cometh out of the mouth, this defileth a man."

Friend, be not deceived; no *liar* will inherit the kingdom of God.

If you struggle with this temptation, just ask God to forgive you and stop lying. Repent of that evil thing and never return to the filth of it. Allow God to cleanse your heart and tongue so new life can flood your soul with the hunger for truth all the days of your temporal life. Remember, there is no such thing as a white lie! A lie is a rotten lie sent from hell, and that, my friend, is no lie!

Micah 2:1 (KJV), "Woe to them that devise iniquity, and work evil upon their beds! when the morning is light, they practise it, because it is in the power of their hand."

Friend, there was an evil injustice that came against my life in the 1990s. I gave myself to diligent search before God concerning the unwanted matter. He spoke these words to me, "I will stop the mouths of the liars as I shut the mouths of the loins in Daniel's day."

Psalm 63:11 (KJV), "But the king shall rejoice in God; every one that sweareth by him shall glory: but the mouth of them that speak lies shall be stopped."

You may want to ask yourself this question: Is a lie worth going to hell for? You may say that is a strong statement; well, let me share with you this strong word of Scripture.

Revelation 21:8 (KJV),

> But the fearful, and unbelieving, and the abominable, and murderers, and whoremongers, and sorcerers, and idolaters, and all liars, shall have their part in the lake which burneth with fire and brimstone: which is the second death.

No one should want to be cast out as a worker of iniquity from before the throne on the day of judgment, but one should want to be addressed by God as a good and faithful servant. We must secure our covenant right to enter into glory through the salvation lifestyle of Jesus Christ and daily walking it out in holiness and reverential fear instead of being deceived and cast into hell for all eternity.

Jesus is coming back for an unspotted bride, not a spotted bride. We must be white and clean, pure and holy, dressed in our white raiment, unspotted from the world and all its tainted wickedness.

CHAPTER 9: THE SUPERNATURAL PHENOMENA OF WISDOM IN THE HEART

Let Wisdom Reign Its Kingdom Identity in You

James 1:5 (KJV), "If any of you lack wisdom, let him ask of God, that giveth to all men liberally, and upbraideth not; and it shall be given him."

Friend, in wisdom, there is no lack, as it is a just weight and perfect balance before the throne.

Many years ago, I was seeking the Lord, and He spoke these words to me, which is an acronym for wisdom:

W—waiting.

I—in.

S—silence.

D—daily.

O—on.

M—me.

Wisdom is a supernatural phenomenon that burns in the heart of God.

God spoke to the prophets of old in wisdom and also to other servants of the Most High in any way that He chose to. His words are truly a phenomenon that no human on planet Earth can fully articulate or understand the profound mysteries of God, as He is supreme, sovereign, and self-governing.

Friend, it's imperative that we seek God's face for the wisdom from above and abide in its holy attributes in the earth. Wisdom is a principal thing; by getting wisdom, we gain greater understanding.

The heart of a wise servant of the Most High God will abide in the constant flow of wisdom from heaven. There is a very high price for the lifestyle of godly wisdom and the strong anointing that comes with this kingdom attribute and many will not choose its straight and narrow path of a suffering lifestyle.

The Beauty of Silence before the Throne

Habakkuk 2:20 (KJV), "But the Lord is in his holy temple: let all the earth keep silence before him."

The Holy Ghost taught me many years ago about the beauty of silence in His holy presence because, in total silence, there is a majestic communing with His glorious truth that cannot be uttered except through a humble and repentant heart that waits in expectancy upon the Lord to speak to His precious child the attributes of His divine nature. There is a melting and molding of the heart in the beauty of silence that burns the wealthy delight of the richness of Scripture insight transformation that takes place in a desperate vessel that fully desires intimacy with the creator of heaven and Earth.

Friend, I want to share with you an experience that I had in my silence before the throne of grace as my heavenly Father was developing rich wisdom in my searching vessel.

He spoke to me to get my Bible and open it up. As I did, I opened to what I called a supernatural word from the Lord because it was just what I was seeking Him about, and the answer came to me in a mighty response of divine intervention. From that time on, I opened my Bible many times to a supernatural word from God. The more we seek His face, the more He reveals to us. God will do the same for you. Have faith.

God loves for us to spend time with Him as it is His requirement for us, and we must make quality time for Him. He richly rewards the searching hearts.

Friend, in learning a life guided by wisdom, I will say this to you:

- Humble yourself before the throne of grace.
- Have your solace time with God. Make time for it. It is required of you.
- Repent of all sin, humble yourself, and ask God to burn out all that is not of His kingdom in your heart; we must be clean vessels, holy and set apart unto the Lord.
- Forgive all that has been done to you.
- Worship Him with all your heart.
- Release your faith with all expectancy and rest in complete trust waiting upon the Lord to commune with you from upon the mercy seat. He will as He chooses.
- Have your Bible and journal or recorder available.
- God will direct a time for you and your spouse to seek His face as well if they are willing and born again.

From Lack to Greater Wisdom and Fulfillment

God is not a God of lack but wealthy in the abundance of wisdom and perfect fulfillment in rewarding completion.

Friend, many lack wisdom and discretion; therefore, many suffer from refusing heaven's salvation plan and wise direction for the abundant life in Jesus Christ, but it doesn't have to be like that at all.

If the heart of a human desires to change as the convicting power of God is convicting one of their sins and drawing them unto the glorious deliverance of Jesus Christ's salvation, and they ask for forgiveness and repent of all their sins, a glorious supernatural phenomenon occurs, and a heart has been set free from Satan's deceptions because there is a constant pulling force trying to drag a soul to the outer darkness of eternal hell, where the worm dieth not.

Friend, when Jesus Christ saves a soul from hell's wicked ways, that soul puts on a new and holy living way through the transforming power of God; therefore, the transformation should be made known in all words and actions of every born-again child of God. The old nature is cast off and placed under your anointed feet and should never return to corrupt and disrupt your new life in Jesus Christ and His abiding nature of heaven on Earth that is a burning force of daily renewal and refreshing to your changed heart.

> Who is a wise man and endued with knowledge among you? let him shew out of a good conversation his works with meekness of wisdom. But if ye have bitter envying and strife in your hearts, glory not, and lie not against the truth. This wisdom descendeth not from above, but is earthly, sensual, devilish. For where envying and strife is, there is confusion and every evil work. But the wisdom that is from above is first pure, then peaceable, gentle, and easy to be intreated, full of mercy and good fruits, without partiality, and without hypocrisy. And the fruit of righteousness is sown in peace of them that make peace.
>
> James 3:13–18 (KJV)

The sweet wisdom from above carries the saved vessel into the holy presence of God and silences the heart for greater character building before the throne of grace in all words and heart actions to be then carried out on the earth as God permits. As children of God, we are to be living examples of godly wisdom from above and not that of the earthly flesh mess that has held many in bondage after the fall of Adam and Eve in the garden in Genesis. The salvation of Jesus freed us from the old, wicked flesh mess of the old man and the old ways under the enslavement to sin. We are in the righteousness of God through Jesus our Lord. Therefore, let us act like it, live like it, and demonstrate our freedom life in Jesus every day as we are an open epistle for all to see and read. May they read us with the writings of *truth* flowing from our anointed lips and compassionate hearts of wealthy purpose that is not of this world of chaos and troubles.

> Till we all come in the unity of the faith, and of the knowledge of the Son of God, unto a perfect man, unto the measure of the stature of the fulness of Christ: That we henceforth be no more children, tossed to and fro, and carried about with every wind of doctrine, by the sleight of men, and cunning craftiness, whereby they lie in wait to deceive; But speaking the truth in love, may grow up into him in all things, which is the head, even Christ: From whom the whole body fitly joined together and compacted by that which every joint supplieth, according to the effectual working in the measure of every part, maketh increase of the body unto the edifying of itself in love. This I say therefore, and testify in the Lord, that ye henceforth walk not as other Gentiles walk, in the vanity of their mind, Having the understanding darkened, being alienated from the life of God through the ignorance that is in them, because of the blindness of their heart: Who being past feeling have given themselves over unto lasciviousness, to work all uncleanness with greediness. But ye have not so learned Christ; If so be that ye have heard him, and have been taught by him, as the truth is in Jesus: That ye put off

concerning the former conversation the old man, which is corrupt according to the deceitful lusts; And be renewed in the spirit of your mind; And that ye put on the new man, which after God is created in righteousness and true holiness. Wherefore putting away lying, speak every man truth with his neighbour: for we are members one of another. Be ye angry, and sin not: let not the sun go down upon your wrath: Neither give place to the devil. Let him that stole steal no more: but rather let him labour, working with his hands the thing which is good, that he may have to give to him that needeth. Let no corrupt communication proceed out of your mouth, but that which is good to the use of edifying, that it may minister grace unto the hearers. And grieve not the holy Spirit of God, whereby ye are sealed unto the day of redemption.

Ephesians 4:13–30 (KJV)

Wisdom is the very holy nature of God that burns the illuminating light of Jesus Christ within the sold-out heart that longs for righteous and holy living on the earth. This kingdom lifestyle can be lived out and walked out through clean vessels of honor surrendered completely to the heavenly Father for His productive purposes.

Friend, wisdom will take you where you have never been, and it will keep you soaring in God, the high and Holy Lord of intimate glory.

In wisdom, one knows the beauty of holiness and sustaining happiness in Jesus Christ.

A life lived in wisdom is a life lived in the abundance of heaven's authentic nature of knowledge and understanding applications and daily practicing the driven force of spiritual insight that brings the soul into the eternal glorious rewards of living a righteous lifestyle while dwelling for a short time upon the earth.

> My son, if thou wilt receive my words, and hide my commandments with thee; So that thou incline thine ear unto wisdom, and apply thine heart to understanding; Yea, if thou criest after knowledge, and liftest up thy voice for understanding; If thou seekest her as silver, and searchest for her as for hid treasures; Then shalt thou understand the fear of the Lord, and find the knowledge of God. For the Lord giveth wisdom: out of his mouth cometh knowledge and understanding. He layeth up sound wisdom for the righteous: he is a buckler to them that walk uprightly. He keepeth the paths of judgment, and preserveth the way of his saints. Then shalt thou understand righteousness, and judgment, and equity; yea, every good path. When wisdom entereth into thine heart, and knowledge is pleasant unto thy soul; Discretion shall preserve thee, understanding shall keep thee.
>
> Proverbs 2:1–11 (KJV)

The Application of Sound Wisdom Identity Realities

Friend, our heavenly Father is making a glorious call to all hearts on the earth to apply wisdom and sound doctrine through Jesus Christ, the all-wise Savior, to the whole world. But who will listen?

Who will heed this urgent call to holy living?

The excellence of the spirit of wisdom is righteous alignment before the throne of grace that pleases the very heart of God and brings perfect balance to the redeemed heart.

Sound wisdom in Hebrew means success. The only sound wisdom for righteous living on the earth is the sound doctrine of the Word of God being revealed and made manifest through Jesus Christ, the living Word, and the very application of the whole Word of God from the book of Genesis chapter 1 through Revelation chapter 22.

Wisdom is character builder, building and transforming the heart through the Word of God so the vessel can apply its guiding principles of anointed transparency that makes the vessel come forth as pure gold before the holy throne of grace.

The beauty of wisdom is the manifestation of heaven's maturity in the sold-out servant's heart that refuses disobedience to God and His Word and also refuses the carnal lifestyle of the fallen nature of mankind. One can abide in the function of wisdom and its strong foundation of pure truth from above and its liberating force that keeps the clean vessel set apart for holiness in the righteous service for advancing the kingdom of God on the earth.

Proverbs 8 is a powerful chapter about wisdom that should stir the searching heart in the reviving fire of heaven's holy desires for clean living and conquering desires for great spiritual success and also success in the natural realm as well. God blesses us in the supernatural realm and the natural realm as well; after all, He is a supernatural Spirit first.

We must seek out God's holy wisdom and apply its holy ways to our lives every day.

His wisdom is profound and without lack or failure. It is an illuminating force of understanding and instructions rewarding hearts with heaven's favor and endless blessings that can never be calculated but only celebrated in the life of Jesus Christ's salvation lifestyle.

> Doth not wisdom cry? and understanding put forth her voice? She standeth in the top of high places, by the way in the places of the paths. She crieth at the gates, at the

entry of the city, at the coming in at the doors.

Proverbs 8:1–3 (KJV)

Proverbs 8:13 (KJV), "The fear of the Lord is to hate evil: pride, and arrogancy, and the evil way, and the froward mouth, do I hate."

Friend, may we say more, "Lord, give us more of You and more of Your Word and wisdom wealth that are priceless treasures from above only revealed from within Your holy heart of eternal love."

We freely partake of Your divine wisdom now, applying it daily to our surrendered vessels so we can share it with the peoples of the earth.

Friend, the Bible is a profound book of God's eternal wisdom, so don't turn its compelling pages away, but open the Word of God and read its impacting words.

The Bible is the powerful, authoritative sword of defense against the wiles of the devil and all his evil works.

"He that committeth sin is of the devil; for the devil sinneth from the beginning. For this purpose the Son of God was manifested, that he might destroy the works of the devil" (1 John 3:8, KJV).

Our own righteousness is as filthy rags; therefore, only in Jesus Christ's righteousness and living in wisdom can we be the overcomers and conquerors that God created us to be. Yes! It's the will of the Father, the way of His nature, and the pure plan of perfection for all saved hearts that want a holy lifestyle while occupying our short time on the earth.

Wisdom is a righteous and holy lifestyle call to all.

A wise word from my heart to you is this: Always say an obedient yes to wisdom and never a rebellious no. Let wisdom rule your heart with the wise kingdom identity realities of the Holy Trinity.

A Wise Heart

The Lord spoke to me that He wanted a mighty shaking in every born-again vessel so they can obtain divine instructions with a holy unction of wise order without fail.

Proverbs 4:7 (KJV), "Wisdom is the principal thing; therefore get wisdom: and with all thy getting get understanding."

Psalm 90:12 (KJV), "So teach us to number our days, that we may apply our hearts unto wisdom."

Friend, a wise heart is a miraculous phenomenon that is characterized by the wise nature of God Himself.

Our days are numbered in the earth, and with an allotted amount of time, we should always strive to apply wisdom and walk therein. You can walk in the wisdom of God as you lay all before the throne of grace. Wisdom is the manifested anointing of heaven in our hearts through Jesus Christ, our wise Savior. We must long to abide in wisdom.

A wise heart is a heart of humble obedience that loves to say yes to the Word of God and His governing will, no matter what others may think.

A wise heart is a listening heart. You can be still before the throne and grow up powerfully in the wisdom of God. Only believe and trust that God will keep you still in fully trusting His truth to purify your humble and contrite heart so that you can reflect the holy identity of Jesus Christ's attributes through your vessel to souls. God will speak to you always within the ordinance of His written Word.

Proverbs 16:16 (KJV), "How much better is it to get wisdom than gold! and to get understanding rather to be chosen than silver!"

A wise heart knows that no amount of money in any global currency or any precious stones or precious metals can compare to the wise anointing that is embedded in the set-apart heart dedicated to service to the master and ministry. No human can purchase the wisdom of God, nor can it be duplicated in the earth. Wisdom is a supernatural wonder of kingdom character in the very attribute of our Holy Father's authenticity. Amen!

Proverbs 19:8 (KJV), "He that getteth wisdom loveth his own soul: he that keepeth understanding shall find good."

A wise heart knows the deep love of God and its wise mandate to accomplish the call to holiness, communicating and demonstrating its kingdom's living realities to people around the globe.

To love our own soul is to have wisdom flowing in a repentant heart and the righteousness of God.

> Many will say to me in that day, Lord, Lord, have we not prophesied in thy name? and in thy name have cast out devils? and in thy name done many wonderful works? And then will I profess unto them, I never knew you: depart from me, ye that work iniquity. Therefore whosoever heareth these sayings of mine, and doeth them, I will liken him unto a wise man, which built his house upon a rock: And the rain descended, and the floods came, and the winds blew, and beat upon that house; and it fell not: for it was founded upon a rock. And every one that heareth these sayings of mine, and doeth them not, shall be likened unto a foolish man, which built his house upon the sand: And the rain descended, and the floods came, and the winds blew, and beat upon that house; and it fell: and great was the fall of it. And it came to pass, when Jesus had ended these sayings, the people were astonished at his doctrine: For he taught them as one having authority, and not as the scribes.
>
> Matthew 7:22–29 (KJV)

A wise heart has a wealthy kingdom foundation of daily applied truths in the glorious Spirit of Jesus Christ. A strong foundation of truth keeps the heart alive in the days of famine and the spirit in the true plumb line of heaven's righteous judgment of the straight and narrow way into heaven's eternity. Let us be like the wise man who built his house upon a rock, and our rock is Jesus Christ. The sweet, plumb line of correction keeps the wise heart in the pure alignment of heaven's divine will and authentic pureness. The foolish desire a crooked life and perverse ways, leaving the heart in the foolish dangers of destruction after destruction.

Ephesians 1:17 (KJV), "That the God of our Lord Jesus Christ, the Father of glory, may give unto you the spirit of wisdom and revelation in the knowledge of him."

A wise heart lives in the illuminating ways of divine revelations that are sent down from above in pure truth and in the holiness of our heavenly Father's agape love.

A wise heart lives in kingdom identity realities.

Friend, to know the all-wise Jesus Christ is to know the Holy Word of God through the illumination and invitation to the spiritual ways of His salvation lifestyle. It's your choice to choose wisdom and truth. Wisdom is a daily invitation to the righteousness of God, so don't allow foolishness to keep you away from the master's feasting place of rich manna and glorious refreshing. The devil is a fool, and he is always wanting to make all humans as he is! Rebuke him and resist his wicked ways. In Jesus' mighty name! Amen!

Friend, may your heart be light with the wisdom of God in these last days as He is calling hearts to sit at His footstool and adhere to His holy ways every day! Oh, the glory life of God's guiding light that shines upon the hearts of humanity, requiring souls to bow at His footstool in willful repentance and holy adoration as the heavenly Father loves to impart wisdom within all humble hearts.

Friend, you must believe daily that God wants to consume your heart and life with the supernatural ways of wisdom's beckoning call. God wants all your heart.

The wisdom of God is a glorious delight. It fashions the heart with the burning hand of God. Its divine nature moves the sold-out heart into the glory realms of greater anointing.

The celebrated splendor of wisdom is timeless and transparent. The mystery of wisdom is eternal, causing the heart of flesh to accept its revealing flow.

The desire for the wisdom of God is delightful to His heart. The search for the wisdom of God is being fully dedicated to the service of Jesus Christ and His discipleship command.

Wisdom burns the love for winning souls deep in the heart, as that is the very breath and life of Jesus Christ.

Proverbs 11:30 (KJV), "The fruit of the righteous is a tree of life; and he that winneth souls is wise."

Friend, I have a word for you: There is a price for wisdom; it costs you everything. Its reward is far above all things in the world. Wisdom will keep your heart and eyes from evil. Wisdom is spiritual success; pursue it with all that is within your vessel, for it shall keep your heart in all godliness. Wisdom subdues the natural mind and safeguards it against the wiles of Satan.

Friend, wisdom is the heartbeat of heaven, and applying wisdom daily to the saved heart is the blessed assurance of arriving and staying forever in glory with God.

CHAPTER 10: A CONSECRATED LIFE UNTO REVERENTIAL FEAR

What God Requires

Deuteronomy 10:12 (KJV),

> And now, Israel, what doth the Lord thy God require of thee, but to fear the Lord thy God, to walk in all his ways, and to love him, and to serve the Lord thy God with all thy heart and with all thy soul.

Reverential fear is a holy way of living, and it's required of all on the earth to live this command in Ecclesiastes chapter 12.

Ecclesiastes 12:13 (KJV), "Let us hear the conclusion of the whole matter: Fear God, and keep his commandments: for this is the whole duty of man."

Friend, as I write this to you today, I want to share with you these words the Lord spoke to me decades ago about holy reverential fear. He said, "Holy fear is the healthy fear before the throne of grace, for the fear of the Lord is to be afraid not to obey My Word."

We all need this holy, healthy fear in the forefront of our hearts and minds as the days are evil.

Wickedness is invading hearts globally with great abominations and hypocrisy, causing hearts to be filled with all manner of wicked deceptions.

Many in the churches today are falling into the dark depths of the ruthless sins of the flesh and totally neglecting the commands of God to abstain from the flesh and its ugliness of enslavement that leaves the heart to a very bitter end of permanent rejection before the throne of God. Hell is always waiting for souls that live in rebellion and constant disobedience to God.

I pray this chapter touches you mightily and sets your mind and heart in the diligent search for a righteous lifestyle of the scripture applications recorded in the Holy Bible from cover to cover.

Let us take a holy fear journey in this chapter together, and I humbly ask that you surrender and humble your heart and mind to the greater enlightenment of these many recorded scriptures, allowing them to pierce your soul with a divine shaking and an awakening of God's very divine order for living holy before His throne. We know that we fall and fail God at times, but my friend, we must repent wholeheartedly and turn away from the sins of the flesh through the power and deliverance of our advocate, Jesus Christ, as we know He shed His blood to set us free and gave us His Word to live by and wear as an armor of light in all righteousness. Therefore, let us dive into the depths of truth that carry our hearts into glory, clean, pure, and holy, shining with the glorious light of Jesus Christ before our heavenly Father's holy throne.

Psalm 103:11 (KJV), "For as the heavens are high above the earth, So great is His mercy toward those who fear Him."

God's mercy is toward those who fear Him, but sadly, many there be who do not fear Him, and many in the churches are falling away from true Christianity and failing to fear God and tremble at His Word. May God have mercy upon us all. The fear of God is a healthy fear that keeps a surrendered heart in the heart center with the Lord and His powerful commands that teach a heart how to live and abide in the presence of God in all holiness and righteousness.

The mercy of the Lord is ready to forgive and ready to save every repentant heart.

There is a grave deception of Satan that is rampant in the world today, which is one can do as they please by living ungodly and unholy and still go to heaven without any accountability.

Leviticus 19:1–2 (KJV), "And the Lord spake unto Moses, saying, Speak unto all the congregation of the children of Israel, and say unto them, Ye shall be holy: for I the Lord your God am holy."

The definition of holy means "dedicated or consecrated to God or a religious purpose; sacred."

Friend, as Christians, our lives should reflect the holy ways of Jesus Christ with every heartbeat and not an occasional representation, but complete consecration. God requires His children to live according to the Scriptures daily, and that is what the lost world needs to see in these last days, but some Christians are living like the world, acting like the world; therefore, they have allowed the enemy to blind their hearts and corrupt their minds. We must live in the heart action of repentance and allow God to transform us into the likeness of His Son Jesus and show the kingdom attributes to the lost and dying world.

I have traveled the world, and in all my global travels, I have witnessed that people are in search of God, His love, and His holy ways being demonstrated in the hearts of true believers shining powerfully in the light of Jesus Christ. We should never look like the world, as Jesus is the light of the world; therefore, we are a light in the darkness that should always illuminate the truth of God and demonstrate it to the hearers. Being an example of Jesus Christ on the earth is the highest honor of all.

God knows our frame, and He remembers that we are dust and that His enduring mercy and divine pity touch the heart and govern our lives as we ask for forgiveness, but friend, we cannot return to the old ways of sin and its corruption of daily destruction. Sin is a stench in God's nostrils, but repentance out of a broken and contrite heart is a sweet aroma before the throne. We are the aroma of Jesus Christ before the throne of grace. We have victory over sin in Jesus Christ, and true repentance is a glorious decision that positions a heart for the blazing force of perpetual holiness as we live in His throne room fire. Note: Hebrews 12:29.

Friend, lost souls everywhere need to see all born-again Christians living a transformed life in Jesus Christ. The filth of the world is vile to our Holy God and His kingdom. We must refuse to return to the vomit of the lustful ways of the flesh and the pride of life. It is deadly and dangerous. Friend, we must strive to look like Jesus, act like Jesus, and live as Jesus did on Earth. We know that He was perfect in nature and without sin, but we also know that by dying daily to our rotten flesh mess, we can live as closely as possible to His divine nature as allowed by our heavenly Father. Amen.

In these last days, some Christians have left their first love and His kingdom lifeways. They are adapting to the lustful desires of sin's stain and open shame to the point that they have lost their identity in Christ and His authentic teachings. They have willfully stepped into wicked compromise, rebellion, and hypocrisy instead of looking like Jesus Christ's divine nature and true holiness.

We need to pray for all Christians and all lost souls across the globe.

Love Me? Reverence Me with Your Whole Heart

Psalm 33:8 (KJV), "Let all the earth fear the Lord: let all the inhabitants of the world stand in awe of him."

Oh, what a glorious plan for all humanity as orchestrated by God above, capturing a humble heart, bringing forth liberation, satisfaction, and transformation for the excellent way of living before His holy presence. The healthy and holy fear brings supernatural salvation, freedom in Jesus Christ, and fulfillment to all who love and serve God wholeheartedly.

Friend, for one to say they are so in love with God after the beautiful salvation experience of being a born-again believer through Jesus Christ shed blood on the cross and having the indwelling Holy Spirit illuminating the heart with the light of truth, there should be an eruption of the reverential fear that carries the heart into the safeguard mode of the heavens holy desires, which holds the saved heart accountable with every living heartbeat.

Matthew 15:8 (KJV), "This people draweth nigh unto me with their mouth, and honoureth me with their lips; but their heart is far from me."

Friend, if one truly and wholeheartedly loves God, there will be evidence of fearing the Holy God of heaven and obeying His perfect law of liberty. It's true that many say they love God but truly do not live for Him, nor do they resist the lust of the flesh, the pride of life, and the carnal ways of the world. All Christians who are living a saved life should be in continuous revival in the heart.

Living to know Him deeply and serving Him completely in all truth and righteousness.

It's simple, and it's a call to action, becoming a wise servant in all the right standings before the throne of grace, where no excuses are allowed and no lies will enter.

God is a consuming fire in Hebrews 10:29, and His all-consuming presence wants to commune with us in a way that is out of the world and in the all-consuming flames of glorious life and supernatural revelation manifestations that cause us to tremble at His Word as every letter is captivating our spiritual vessel and bursting forth the kingdom identity realities that overtake our mind, our will, our emotions, and whole heart! There is such a powerful life force of intimate joy and holy glory as we draw nigh to God in our love walk unto Him in reverential fear.

Friend, I pray these words deeply touch your heart and move your spirit to a higher calling and deeper intimacy with our heavenly Holy Father.

Fear Me, My Child

Fear Me, My child, and I will reveal more of My heart to you.

Fear Me, and you will walk out in great success in the service of the king.

Fear Me, and I will take you where you've never dreamed.

Fear Me, and I will show you the many ramparts of My presence.

Fear Me, for I will keep your heart holy and clean before Me.

Fear Me, and I will anoint thee with greater wisdom dominion.

Fear Me, and I will pour out the continual flowing of the burning oil of gladness.

Fear Me, and I will keep you in the rich discernment and royal delight.

Fear Me, and I will unfold wealthy secrets that were set apart just for you.

Fear Me, and I will raise you up in the greater works mission mandate before My Son.

Fear Me, and I will always speak profoundly to your surrendered and expectant vessel.

Fear Me, and I will teach you how to stand before kings and not be ashamed.

Fear Me, and I will guide you into the fiery treasury of My unconquerable truths.

Fear Me, and I will reveal My supernatural self to you in greater wonders.

Fear Me, and I give unto you My escaping grace and unhindered favor that last a lifetime.

Fear Me, and I will cause thee to rest in the holy assurance of My Son's wealthy inheritance of the high price through His salvation.

Fear not, for I love sharing holy intimacy with you in My throne room presence of eternal love and righteousness.

Fear Me, My love, My bride, and I will perform all the promises that I have spoken to you; not one of them will fall to the ground, but all shall be fulfilled before My throne.

Fear Me, and I will cause all your enemies to lick the dust under your feet.

Fear Me, for I have power to keep your heart and keep your soul out of hell.

Fear Me, and I will consume your heart and greatly commune with you in the throne room of My intimate grace.

My child, I patiently wait for your heart to come into My presence.

I love burning your heart with the fiery depths of My holy love.

Isaiah 66:2 (KJV), "For all those things hath mine hand made, and all those things have been, saith the Lord: but to this man will I look, even to him that is poor and of a contrite spirit, and trembleth at my word."

Psalm 115:11 (KJV), "Ye that fear the Lord, trust in the Lord: he is their help and their shield."

Friend, the wise beauty in fearing the Lord is the reality of being before His holy throne where everything in spirit and truth is true holiness and righteousness, and that is what God plans for our daily lives to be while occupying this temporal earth.

We must become holy as Jesus our Lord is holy. Make no mistake about it, as the sure mercies of God want our lives lived in the holy heartbeat of heaven! The very heartbeat of heaven is that we can intimately know the heart of God the Father, as that is His perfect plan and perfect will for our lives.

Jesus Christ gave you the holy and loyal opportunity to be holy as He is through His death on the cross. You are worthy to receive the greater depths of spiritual growth and increased anointing, as Jesus Christ became sin for you so you could be made righteous in Him. Don't listen to the ways of the devil and the carnal ways of false religions. You must 100 percent believe that you can live a holy life on Earth and refuse to live under the old fallen nature of Adam and Eve and the grave deceptions of hell and all false religions.

"For he hath made him to be sin for us, who knew no sin; that we might be made the righteousness of God in him" (2 Corinthians 5:21, KJV).

The very essence of a Spirit-filled life is a chartered course characterized by the mercy of God and the compassion of Jesus whereby one can be established on the wise foundation of the Holy Spirit's truth and righteous leading through a free will choice of daily surrender.

God has a holy path of pure truth before you. The world paves crooked ways before souls.

God wants all to bow at His holy footstool. The devil wants all enslaved to sin and its destructive lifestyle.

God wants us with Him for all eternity. The devil wants to torment souls in hell for all eternity. The more we die to our old carnal ways, the more God gives us His holy ways!

Friend, choose salvation and holiness, and reap the everlasting peace and happiness in heaven!

Reverential fear is a profound action of a humble and repentant heart; it moves the heart of God to pleasures of righteousness in the glorious attributes of His divine nature.

A Holy Militant Duty

Friend, a holy militant duty before the throne of God is knowing that you have been saved into a salvation covenant that is a serious call to righteousness, leaving all the carnal ways of the flesh by placing them daily under your anointed feet so that you richly live in your kingdom identity reality of reverential fear and carry out your designed destiny with a strong anointing in the service of the master.

God wants all saved hearts surrendered unto Him so the end-time gospel works of Jesus Christ will be fulfilled in all power and glory as souls need to be saved twenty-four seven, 365 days a year.

Proverbs 15:33 (KJV), "The fear of the Lord is the instruction of wisdom; and before honour is humility."

We must display our anointed vessel in the humble confidence of Jesus Christ our Lord as we rise and move in the honor of heaven so hearts can see that it is Jesus Christ in us, the true anointed one, and all praise, glory, and honor belongs to Him! God loves to honor us, and we must learn to flow in these kingdom attributes as it is heaven's working and planning within our hearts and that not of ourselves! Amen.

Proverbs 14:26 (KJV), "In the fear of the Lord is strong confidence: and his children shall have a place of refuge."

Proverbs 16:6 (KJV), "By mercy and truth iniquity is purged: and by the fear of the Lord men depart from evil."

Our heavenly Father has required His mighty Christian soldiers to depart from evil and apply the wisdom in reverential fire to come forth shining in the light of truth before all people and step out in holy boldness, being unashamed of the gospel of Jesus Christ and His wise words of life. Friend, we must be a beacon of hope and well-established in spirit and truth, allowing nothing to get in the way. All peoples of the earth need the living hope in us, especially seeing us striving to live holy unto the Lord!

Psalm 25:14 (KJV), "The secret of the Lord is with them that fear him; and he will shew them his covenant."

God is a revealer of His covenant, and His secrets are endless, but for those who truly fear Him and keep His commands, He is faithful to reveal more of His hidden manna to all who seek Him out with reverential fear, paving the way in holiness and righteous living. A servant of righteousness lives in the fruits of the Spirit and the leading of the Spirit, partaking of the divine nature of Jesus Christ Himself. This is the perfect plan for your life, and in the unfolding of the Scriptures, there is a forming of Jesus Christ's likeness that keeps your heart burning for more holiness and detesting the carnal ways of the old sinful nature. Friend, it's so exciting to live in the reverential fear of God and walk out the divine nature of Jesus Christ, His Son.

Let's take this time and ask God to reveal great and mighty things to us as we daily acknowledge that He wants our hearts before His throne and awaiting holy assignments for the greater good of His kingdom realities to be manifested on the earth. God loves to show us His covenant truth and walk us out in the militant promises of His holy love wonders as friend to friend and being the happy servants in the workmanship of Jesus Christ our Lord.

A Constant Accountability in Reverential Fear

Psalm 112:1 (KJV), "Praise ye the Lord. Blessed is the man that feareth the Lord, that delighteth greatly in his commandments."

Friend, in the consecrated lifestyle of having reverential fear in God, we greatly adhere to His holy and loving commands with willful obedience to find great delight in the sacred Scriptures. In doing so, our daily growth process and spiritual performance become greater in the sweet assurance of heaven's wisdom to live according to all that is daily required of us. Friend, live on in holiness, and move forward in the accelerations of the heavenly Father's greater glory realm, where constant accountability is a sweet savor before His throne.

> Now thanks be unto God, which always causeth us to triumph in Christ, and maketh manifest the savour of his knowledge by us in every place. For we are unto God a sweet savour of Christ, in them that are saved, and in them that perish.
>
> 2 Corinthians 2:14–15 (KJV)

Remember, constant accountability keeps the heart burning with greater demonstrations of tangible spirit life within your anointed vessel. Every day should be a self-examination of the heart condition. It's always a heart issue condition before the throne. Amen!

The miracle of reverential fear in God for me is living in the wisdom of the constant heart search of being as God wants me to be and exemplifying it in my daily walk, showing the world an excellent way to live in the wisdom and life force of the kingdom of God without any evidence of the devil ruling and corrupting my created vessel. For me, being led by the Holy Spirit keeps my heart in the burning torch of the liberty life force, where I see nothing but my God before me. This allows His kingdom lifeways to constantly transform my heart into the glorious greatness of His daily plans for the good of my Spirit-filled, Spirit-fed, and Spirit-led life! Oh, what sweet surrender in the accountability splendor of holiness and His all-consuming loveliness; there is no want and no lack before the throne of grace, the holy accountable place!

Psalm 34:9 (KJV), "O fear the Lord, ye his saints: for there is no want to them that fear him."

Proverbs 28:14 (KJV), "Happy is the man that feareth alway: but he that hardeneth his heart shall fall into mischief."

Friend, I have many scriptures in this chapter and much-needed ones, I must say, for we all need daily Word reminders. To be honest, writing this book for you is most pleasing for me, but the greatest pleasure I have in these written words is the sacred scriptures of the Holy Word. We need the Word of God to become so deeply embedded within our souls. I am a woman of the Word, and I love sharing the Word! It's my kingdom identity. Friend, we can pick up many wonderful inspirational books, but there is nothing, and I mean nothing, like picking the one and only Book and opening it to the very heartbeat of God and receiving His truths with an open heart, open mind, and open spirit. Oh, how we desperately need a deep hunger and thirst for truth daily!

Proverbs 14:27 (KJV), "The fear of the Lord is a fountain of life, to depart from the snares of death."

Friend, in the fountain of life, we see life and beauty in all holiness where the glorious life flows, making all hearts live in the overflow of righteousness, peace, and joy in the Holy Ghost, which is the glorious atmosphere of heaven. Note: Romans 14:17; Psalm 36:9.

Psalm 97:10 (KJV), "Ye that love the Lord, hate evil: he preserveth the souls of his saints; he delivereth them out of the hand of the wicked."

Friend, God is a mighty deliverer! I have witnessed God's mighty deliverance in my personal life throughout my whole life as I know you have witnessed His greatness manifest in your midst. Every time I begin to ponder His holy wonders and faithfulness, it erupts a jubilant force of unending thankfulness and praise and how noteworthy God's stability is in our lives. God is always performing a live recording in our hearts. May we always be attentive to His workings with reverential fear on the forefront of our hearts and minds with the expectations that greater illuminations of truth will spring forth like the noonday sun, causing us to carry the flaming torch of heaven with the perfection of holy endurance and captivating performance in our destiny identity of Jesus Christ liberty lifestyle.

Psalm 19:9 (KJV), "The fear of the Lord is clean, enduring for ever: the judgments of the Lord are true and righteous altogether."

Friend, allow God to make a clean sweep in your heart today, taking all the filth of the carnal ways away and starting afresh with new heartbeats of His rewarding, righteous ways! A clean and holy heart will enter heaven with great rewards and endless treasures! Note: See Psalm 51:10.

God has the perfect highway of holiness paved with His glorious attributes that we can delight in and demonstrate powerfully to the world! Friend, get busy about the Father's business in wisdom and righteousness, for souls are awaiting your holy arrival in great power and demonstrations! When a sold-out heart truly wants to please the Lord, it will richly be in a living state of obedience to take on the powerful purposes ordained by our heavenly Father so it can fulfill its designed destiny in holiness and with powerful anointed demonstration manifestation.

When we live in the fear of the Lord, the anointing will never leave our hearts and lives. Keeping our first love first is the atmosphere of heaven. Always give God first place in your life, and you will never be without a lack of mercy in your heart!

Luke 1:50 (KJV), "And his mercy is on them that fear him from generation to generation."

Heart's Full of Reverential Fear

The Holy Desire of the Five Wise Virgins

Friend, there is such a powerful message in these verses of the Scriptures. I pray that God touches your heart with the fiery oil of Jesus Christ's divine nature as you read these impacting words of the Holy desire of five wise virgins who had their hearts, visions, and whole vessels full of truth and living in the daily expectation that a bridegroom was coming for them. They *all* knew their required actions of wisdom were only to readily please the bridegroom, as their hearts were in great expectation, awaiting their bridegroom with glorious spiritual preparedness.

What a holy acceptance came forth from the heart of the bridegroom to the wise virgins.

> Then shall the kingdom of heaven be likened unto ten virgins, which took their lamps, and went forth to meet the bridegroom. And five of them were wise, and five were foolish. They that were foolish took their lamps, and took no oil with them: But the wise took oil in their vessels with their lamps. While the bridegroom tarried, they all slumbered and slept. And at midnight there was a cry made, Behold, the bridegroom cometh; go ye out to meet him. Then all those virgins arose, and trimmed their lamps. And the foolish said unto the wise, Give us of your oil; for our lamps are gone out. But the wise answered, saying, Not so; lest there be not enough for us and you: but go ye rather to them that sell, and buy for yourselves. And while they went to buy, the bridegroom came; and they that were ready went in with him to the marriage: and the door was shut. Afterward came also the other virgins, saying, Lord, Lord, open to us. But he answered and said, Verily I say unto you, I know you not. Watch therefore, for ye know neither the day nor

the hour wherein the Son of man cometh.

Matthew 25:1–13 (KJV)

The foolish virgins could not have the wise virgins' oil. It was not permitted! Being unprepared when the bridegroom cometh will be a horrifying sight to behold. Every hour of every day is to be an hour of wise readiness. Get ready today.

Friend, our heavenly Father gave to us the holy bridegroom, Jesus Christ, to receive us unto Himself through the salvation transformation lifestyle, having our hearts consumed with the anointing from on high. When we see our Lord face to face, and we forever inherit His kingdom of glory, it will be a glorious time for all eternity. May I say to you today, have your heart right with God and your vessel full of reverential fear and holiness, ready to be in the very anointed presence of your heavenly bridegroom, the forever reigning king of glory!

What a beautiful, holy desire that came into fruition for the wise virgins that we read of today. We must always be ready to meet the Lord and occupy abundantly until He comes to take us home. Amen.

Trained in Reverential Fear

Psalm 111:10 (KJV), "The fear of the Lord is the beginning of wisdom: a good understanding have all they that do his commandments: his praise endureth for ever."

Friend, living life consecrated unto the Word of God is truly lived wisely before the throne of God. The fear of God is an attribute of wisdom.

Deuteronomy 5:29 (KJV), "O that there were such an heart in them, that they would fear me, and keep all my commandments always, that it might be well with them, and with their children for ever!"

Friend, for me, as a child growing up, my mother taught my three brothers and me about the fear of God and how it is a way of life never to be ignored or taken lightly but literally concerning the welfare of our eternal life, as God has provided instructions for all to live by in His Holy Word. She taught us that the Bible was holy, every single word, jot, and tittle. I had a fear of God in not wanting to go to hell, that's for sure, but the enemy wanted to destroy my life, and he made that known as the tempter came with his wicked attacks. I suffered for my sin, and we all have messed up. I assure you, I have failed God in my life, but I am not that person today because the more hell was attacking, the greater the Lord was convicting my heart. I praise God for His convicting power and saving grace, and that hell does not rule my life and heart! Amen!

Conviction is glorious in its spiritual quest to change our hearts and save us from Satan's hell; it is incomprehensible and miraculous indeed.

I love the leadership of the Holy Trinity and how God harmonizes so powerfully with His Son, Jesus, and His Holy Spirit, paving the holy way for our saved lives to abide in the perpetual flame of holy education and greater advancements in the Godhead. God's deity does not change, nor does our identity in Jesus Christ, as we stay in fellowship with the Trinity in reverential fear!

Friend, living in the perfect will of God in reverential fear is drawing from the wealthy wellspring of the wisdom in Jesus Christ! Amen and amen!

I delight in this beautiful childhood memory of when my father would take us way back into a Kentucky Hollow on his cousin's property, and I loved playing in the creek. Just above the creek, there was a spring of water that was so beautiful in the way that it flowed over the rocks, and it looked so crystal clear. As I was looking at it one day, my father said that I could take a drink of the freshwater, so I did, and it was delightful to taste.

Wisdom is like a bubbling brook, and the fear of God is a life force that sustains us in the living water of Jesus, our Lord! Wisdom and fear of the Lord are covenant partners of 100 percent unified harmony and wholeness in the supreme authority that imparts the anointing to the saved and sold-out heart.

Philippians 2:12 (KJV), "Wherefore, my beloved, as ye have always obeyed, not as in my presence only, but now much more in my absence, work out your own salvation with fear and trembling."

We have a perfect instruction from Paul, the apostle, to always stay in obedience to God twenty-four seven, 365 days a year, as well as working out our own salvation in reverential fear, knowing that God wants us completely trained up in the fortitude of His authority and powerful anointing of Jesus Christ.

Friend, God's perfect will for us is to walk out our salvation in authenticity and integrity that pours forth like a wellspring of life before all hearers! Amen!

Psalm 86:11 (KJV), "Teach me thy way, O Lord; I will walk in thy truth: unite my heart to fear thy name."

Proverbs 10:27 (KJV), "The fear of the Lord prolongeth days: but the years of the wicked shall be shortened."

The Healthy Fear Turns a Soul Away from Hell

The devil comes against the flesh to corrupt the heart and mind. Only God Almighty has the power and authority over every single human that has ever been created. He has the authority to cast a soul into hell. Friend, I always say these words: don't get caught dead without Jesus Christ. Fearing God is a fountain of wisdom that keeps one living holy and always ready to step into eternity with the full acceptance of God, the Holy Father, and His eternal reward of heaven itself. Oh, do you see the imperative importance of living in holiness?

Don't allow the devil to deceive you into thinking that a lukewarm lifestyle is accepted before the holy throne of grace. Be quick to repent and live out your precious days as God desires and not that of self-centeredness and demanding ways.

"And fear not them which kill the body, but are not able to kill the soul: but rather fear him which is able to destroy both soul and body in hell" (Matthew 10:28, KJV).

> And I say unto you my friends, Be not afraid of them that kill the body, and after that have no more that they can do. But I will forewarn you whom ye shall fear: Fear him, which after he hath killed hath power to cast into hell; yea, I say unto you, Fear him.
>
> Luke 12:4–5 (KJV)

"Having therefore these promises, dearly beloved, let us cleanse ourselves from all filthiness of the flesh and spirit, perfecting holiness in the fear of God" (2 Corinthians 7:1, KJV).

"He will fulfil the desire of them that fear him: he also will hear their cry, and will save them" (Psalm 145:19, KJV).

CHAPTER 11:
IT'S GOD'S CREATED PLAN, NOT OURS

An Authentic Plan, Not Ours

Jeremiah 29:11 (KJV), "For I know the thoughts that I think toward you, saith the Lord, thoughts of peace, and not of evil, to give you an expected end."

God's authentic plan moves the humble heart with all diligence to the expectant place of higher callings and spiritual capabilities that surpass all limitations and onslaughts of hell. You can walk out the plans and purposes of God because it's God's plan for you and not your own. One thing about God: His plans for you can never be thwarted by any devil or any human.

Friend, you must live in the anointing, speak in the anointing, and walk forth in the anointing in great demonstrations of power. God's thoughts toward you are more than can be numbered, and He is waiting to share many kingdom thoughts.

I want to share with you an experience that I had with the Lord many years ago. I was driving on Interstate 94 in Michigan when the Lord suddenly spoke these words to me, "I have longed for so long to share these things with you, My child." I had a powerful revelation on the desire of God's heart to share many things with me and how He longs so deeply to share His heart with all His children. He is just waiting so patiently and compassionately for our willful surrender and desires for us to sit at His feet and receive glorious things already abiding within His holy heart. The truth is

God longs to share more with us than we could ever begin to ask Him for or thank Him for or, for that matter, to even praise Him for.

Job 42:2 (KJV), "I know that thou canst do every thing, and that no thought can be withholden from thee."

Friend, may we begin this chapter together in the fear of the Lord and in the readiness of mind as we enter the presence of the master feasting place with a cheerful heart of hunger for greater depths of His presence and higher heights in His profound anointing.

I want to share with you the glorious kingdom identity reality of settling into the selfless mode and a discipline and determined lifestyle in Jesus Christ our Lord, which is a lifestyle of resting in the full assurance of His leading and learning how to flee the old selfishness of the rotten flesh mess that hinders the heart and stifles the growth process of a child of God.

Let me share with you my journey of His authentic plan that is established within my heart.

Friend, many years ago, the Lord spoke to me about my heart being like a writing tablet before His throne. When we repent, He wipes the tablet of our heart completely clean and makes it ready for new recordings from His heart. For you see, friend, the devil is always ready to accuse you of all those sins and past sins that perhaps you recorded on the writing tablet of your heart, and you have suffered torment and heavy troubles because of the darkness of sin. However, my friend, you must always keep this in your heart and mind: when God forgives a heart of confessed sins, clean is the condition of the heart to start afresh with new mercies every morning, and that is good gospel news!

Our heavenly Father's faithfulness envelopes you with new developments of higher kingdom education as sin has been daily defeated and crushed under your anointed feet!

Remember, God's personal plan for you is always genuinely filled with destiny purpose that only you can fulfill in Jesus Christ's identity manifested in the one and only unique you!

Lamentations 3:22–23 (KJV), "It is of the Lord's mercies that we are not consumed, because his compassions fail not. They are new every morning: great is thy faithfulness."

His Authentic Molding

I love the beauty in God's molding power that manifests right in our surrendered hearts.

Friend, no matter our age in this life, there is a potter's wheel that we must remain on, if you will. The allotted days of our lives are not ours to fashion; therefore, we must remain pliable to the master's holy hands and stay in His safe hands! God is about partnership and covenant relationship with His children, so it's vitally important as a child of God to never go ahead of him because the Holy Spirit is the wondrous paraclete that is alongside us. The Holy Spirit also lives inside our hearts when we become born again.

Many people want to be formed and molded by the way of the fallen nature and the dusty mess of the world instead of the purity of truth and living a sacrificed and sanctified life in Jesus Christ, meaning making holy in a simple nature. God wants to take our dusty frames and fashion us through the transforming power of the divine nature of Jesus Christ as the workmanship of His glory. Life is simple in the fact that we go from our mother's womb to the potter's wheel. We had to leave the womb to be born; now, we have to stay on the potter's wheel to be daily transformed in God's created likeness to live right on the earth. God's thought toward you is: Can I do with you as the potter did with the clay?

> The word which came to Jeremiah from the Lord, saying, Arise, and go down to the potter's house, and there I will cause thee to hear my words. Then I went down

to the potter's house, and, behold, he wrought a work on the wheels. And the vessel that he made of clay was marred in the hand of the potter: so he made it again another vessel, as seemed good to the potter to make it. Then the word of the Lord came to me, saying, O house of Israel, cannot I do with you as this potter? saith the Lord. Behold, as the clay is in the potter's hand, so are ye in mine hand, O house of Israel. At what instant I shall speak concerning a nation, and concerning a kingdom, to pluck up, and to pull down, and to destroy it; If that nation, against whom I have pronounced, turn from their evil, I will repent of the evil that I thought to do unto them. And at what instant I shall speak concerning a nation, and concerning a kingdom, to build and to plant it; If it do evil in my sight, that it obey not my voice, then I will repent of the good, wherewith I said I would benefit them. Now therefore go to, speak to the men of Judah, and to the inhabitants of Jerusalem, saying, Thus saith the Lord; Behold, I frame evil against you, and devise a device against you: return ye now every one from his evil way, and make your ways and your doings good. And they said, There is no hope: but we will walk after our own devices, and we will every one do the imagination of his evil heart.

Jeremiah 18:1–12 (KJV)

God spoke to Jeremiah to go down to the potter's house. He wanted Jeremiah's obedience and listening ear. God wanted Jeremiah to hear His words. The potter was making something at the wheel. Friend, I always say this referring to Ezekiel's vision in Ezekiel 1: As wheels move, so are we moving in motion, and so is life moving from the beginning of time up until the last day on Earth. We stay in the motion of the wheel with Him and, like the prophets, know Him deeply in the consuming truth.

Friend, in Jeremiah chapter 18 and verse 2, we see where the potter made a marred vessel, so he made it again into another vessel; that was wise of the potter to do. In verse six, God begins to speak, saying, "O house of Israel, can I not do with you as this potter?" (NKJV).

Friend, God is fed up with what some carnal clay of the old carnal ways that flesh has made, and He will destroy all the marred works of the carnal flesh in an instant, which is for our good and, just like in verse seven, referring to the nation of Israel, to pluck up, pull down, and to destroy it. God wants to destroy everything that the flesh has created without the divine order of His destiny identity design for our own personal lives. All self-made kingdoms end up in a heap of rubble and a marred mess. God is doing great and mighty things, big things, because the harvest field is going to be flooded with souls that need to be harvested before the catching away of the bride. God loves molding a heart into His kingdom's likeness, and He loves for us to be like the oaks of righteousness in Isaiah 61:3 (KJV),

> To appoint unto them that mourn in Zion, to give unto them beauty for ashes, the oil of joy for mourning, the garment of praise for the spirit of heaviness; that they might be called trees of righteousness, the planting of the Lord, that he might be glorified.

Friend, as the mighty oaks are powerful in strength, so may we be strong in the hand of the Lord, our mighty potter and *dunamis* creator, who is creating greater glory in our surrender vessels as we stay upon His fiery wheel that burns sweet anointed life in our molded vessels of honor being deeply rooted in the Word so our hearts are established in wise covenant. Truly, our hearts are vessels of honor before the Father.

In Jeremiah 17:7–10 (KJV),

> Blessed is the man that trusteth in the Lord, and whose hope the Lord is. For he shall be as a tree planted by the waters, and that spreadeth out her roots by the river, and shall not see when heat cometh, but her leaf shall be green; and shall not be careful in the year of drought, neither shall cease from yielding fruit. The heart is deceitful above all things, and desperately wicked: who can know it? I the Lord search the heart, I try the reins, even to give every man according to his ways, and according to the fruit of his doings.

We are in His hand, so it's imperative that we remain there! Friend, when we keep our hearts on the potter's wheel for God to authentically mold, there will be no evil to remain in our hearts as we are being daily purged and consumed by the fiery hand of God!

We must refuse all wickedness in Jesus' mighty name! Amen!

Friend, some people, in their evil ways of pride, refuse the potter's wheel and take control of their own lives; they also want control of everything, period! They want to manipulate the wheel. This evil behavior is a work of hell and will only end up in self-destruction. God will not permit a heart to behave in such evil practices without exposure, consequences, and open shame!

The enemy wants Christians to return to the ways of the world and from serving the one true living God. The devil wants all deceived and bound by religious deceptions of very kind. Let God fashion your heart with the holy fire of heaven so that you will not desire your own way.

Friend, the heart can be so desperately wicked, as recorded in Jeremiah 17, because many souls have no reverential fear of God. We must choose obedience and be fashioned by God into the greatness of the reflection of Jesus Christ. God is raising up a remnant that is endowed with great power, one pure in heart and holy in servanthood to the master.

Refuse the Potter's Wheel and Arrogance Will Manifest

When arrogance gets in the way and refuses the potter's wheel, this is what takes place in the heart. The selfish nature of the rotten flesh mess will be rebellious before God.

A self-made kingdom will be taken into captivity because of unholy practices in the ugliness of arrogance, causing the flesh dominance to always prevent the heart from fully submitting in complete surrender to God in whole-hearted repentance. Instead, there will always be the invading deeds of crippling darkness where the heart becomes imprisoned to its own self-destruction. But there is hope because God specializes in revealing the condition of our hearts because we should be willing to stay on the potter's wheel of refining purification and authenticity! Self-examination of the heart should be a daily practice and always at the forefront of every born-again believer's heart and mind.

Friend, let the living water of Jesus Christ fashion your heart into the eternal flow of the living proof of His holy truth as we are His open epistle before the world to see and read! May they read well as the anointed flow of heaven is burning purity in our hearts before all peoples!

God has never fashioned a marred vessel; He fashions a holy vessel to carry His glory and further demonstrate His power to the world. He wants to reign in the heart and the vessel so it will become honorable. Friend, just remember one of the worst enemies is what you look at in the mirror, which I call the flesh mess of self. It is very dangerous and detrimental when the flesh has no self-control but is parading around out of control, bullying people, and trying to play God and rule over many lives with lies and manipulations that are driven by rebellion and the nature of Lucifer.

The end of this type of behavior is described in the next several verses in 2 Timothy chapter 2.

> Nevertheless the foundation of God standeth sure, having this seal, The Lord knoweth them that are his. And, let every one that nameth the name of Christ depart from iniquity. But in a great house there are not only vessels of gold and of silver, but also of wood and of earth; and some to honour, and some to dishonour. If a man therefore purge himself from these, he shall be a vessel unto honour, sanctified, and meet for the master's use, and prepared unto every good work. Flee also youthful lusts: but follow righteousness, faith, charity, peace, with them that call on the Lord out of a pure heart. But foolish and unlearned questions avoid, knowing that they do gender strifes. And the servant of the Lord must not strive; but be gentle unto all men, apt to teach, patient, In meekness instructing those that oppose themselves; if God peradventure will give them repentance to the acknowledging of the truth; And that they may recover themselves out of the snare of the devil, who are taken captive by him at his will.
>
> 2 Timothy 2:19–26 (KJV)

Friend, we are in the last days, and it's time to make things right down here before we leave the earth and stand before God in heaven because we can't make it right on that noble day of accountability! People desperately need God and His holy ways to make it in these last and evil days. Amen.

For us to richly desire becoming a vessel of honor, we must be purged of the wicked ways of sin, allowing the holy fire of heaven that burns with a holy blaze of purification and transformation so our master can create a masterpiece before His throne of grace.

We must go more and more into the Word, prayer, and worship so the shining display of heaven's attributes reigns the noble cause and mandates of all the set-apart work of the kingdom that God has for us to accomplish. God desires to supernaturally build us and increase us day after day in His Word and Spirit. We must step forth as the remnant of holiness because the powers of hell are invading some hearts with the most demonized, demoralized, desensitized, and perverted things in our nation, and they're demanding it to be that way.

I have kingdom of God news for the world and for the devil. A remnant army of righteousness is dismantling hell in Jesus' name! We have faithfully stayed on the potter's wheel, and the fiery molding hand of God has burned hell's ways out of our flesh. The holy fire of truth has transformed our hearts into the holy love fire desires of the glory fire of authenticity and the holy display of divine favor and the victorious authority that can never be defeated! We are mighty oaks that are the planting of the Lord to defy the devil, with the blood sword of the Lord piercing demons at every turn!

> For we preach not ourselves, but Christ Jesus the Lord; and ourselves your servants for Jesus' sake. For God, who commanded the light to shine out of darkness, hath shined in our hearts, to give the light of the knowledge of the glory of God in the face of Jesus Christ. But we have this treasure in earthen vessels, that the excellency of the power may be of God, and not of us. We are troubled on every side, yet not distressed; we are perplexed, but not in despair; Persecuted, but not forsaken; cast down, but not destroyed; Always bearing about in the body the dying of the Lord Jesus, that the life also of Jesus might be made manifest in our body. For we which live are always delivered unto death for Jesus' sake, that the life also of Jesus might be made manifest in our mortal flesh.
>
> 2 Corinthians 4 5–11 (KJV)

We've been persecuted over and over. Some of us feel like we have been out in a wilderness and desert, and of course, we've been as a lamb to the slaughter multiple times. We've been accused of things that were not so, but praise God; we have kingdom reputation in Jesus Christ and His revelation of spiritual insight and resurrection power and His vindication and restitution. Our identity is in Jesus Christ, our defining Lord of glory. The potter (God) defines the vessel of honor that He created when His hand has formed, molded, and transformed the vessel unto the likeness of His Son.

Friend, the treasures that be of God in our earthen vessels are the demonstration of Word empowerments through Jesus Christ and the Holy Spirit burning the kingdom identity realities in all sold-out vessels before the peoples in the earth. Amen!

God loves to take fragile jars of clay containing these treasures and use all vessels for His radiant glory. Friend, do you see why the devil wants you to take control of your life and not remain in the pliable place upon the potter's wheel?

Remember, with total submission to the potter, there will always be rich revealing of God speaking directly to your heart, and you will celebrate applying the sacred Scriptures as there will always be an increase in your wisdom and anointing!

May your words come to life as the burning force of heaven churns your heart into the lavishness of purity and holiness in all the moldings of heaven's masterpiece that is formed by the great and mighty power of God in grace and special favor! Oh, what glory in the saved heart of a vessel fit for the master's use!

Only a foolish vessel refuses pure truth, having the heart dictated by evil, creating their own marred vessel in wicked pride that will be denied in the end before the throne of God.

May I make this plea to thee?

Repent, repent while there is still time! God loves you, and He doesn't want to throw the clay away. Oh no, my friend. God wants to take your clay and make you into a beautiful vessel before His throne.

The Formed Nature of Jesus Christ in the Heart

What God formed and created in me is not formed and created in you. Don't be deceived by Satan because you cannot be anyone else. I am Sherry, and you are you. Yes, Jesus lives within saved hearts just as Paul had his own authenticity in his destiny identity in Jesus Christ, and so did Peter and others mention throughout the Word. Be what God alone called you to be: your unique self in Jesus Christ and His creative flow in the anointing! No two fingerprints are alike, and no two snowflakes are alike.

The Writing Tablet of Daily Mercies

Proverbs 7:1–3 (KJV),

> My son, keep my words, and lay up my commandments with thee. Keep my commandments, and live; and my law as the apple of thine eye. Bind them upon thy fingers, write them upon the table of thine heart.

Every day is filled with new heartbeats; every day, God wants to write new things on the tablets of our hearts through His Word and Spirit. Let your heart be ready to hear and receive.

The commands of God are fiery truths that want to consume every human's heart on Earth. The Word was written for all of mankind! The heart of God's mercy loves to record upon the tablets of our humble hearts the revelations of His kingdom.

Let us take a journey in the Lord and allow Him to bring peace, harmony, happiness, and a majestic mandate into the hearts of every born-again believer who has an ear to hear and a heart to receive.

The writing tablet of daily mercies is ready for the recorded words flowing down from the authentic author and finisher of our faith. The words are already recorded in the heart of the heavenly Father.

Every word that is purposed to be recorded in the humble and repentant heart of the believer will establish a far more holy love fire desire to listen to and receive the kingdom plans that are always being made manifest in the hearts of true worshippers.

Your Writings of Burning Truth

Jeremiah 20:9 (KJV),

> Then I said, I will not make mention of him, nor speak any more in his name. But his word was in mine heart as a burning fire shut up in my bones, and I was weary with forbearing, and I could not stay.

Friend, when God brings a word to the heart, it is a fiery word that is always with acceleration, fueled by the glory of God and His reigning fiery force of liberation and revelation.

Revelation acceleration is always stirring the heart for the greater advancements of the kingdom of God for the gospel's sake.

Friend, in the many, many years that I've drawn new life from the presence of God and His Holy Word, I have swiftly accelerated in His glorious anointing that has always kept me set apart and guarded for heaven's creative work of the ministry depths that are always unfolding in my vessel. As my heart is before the face of God at His throne and my heart tablet is free for His recordings and depositaries. I AM that I AM is my recorded way, as I am completely out of His holy way! Remember, friend, the flesh and selfish ambitions always speak empty words with empty plans; thus, there is no anointing on the lives of evil intentions and evil motives! Amen. God's Word is plain; He resisteth the proud but gives grace to the humble. Note: James 4:6.

God is always desiring to write on the tablets of our pure hearts.

His holy fire is upon my tongue, and the release of His recorded truth from within my heart is the force of freedom and freedom of kingdom speech that cannot be quenched but is the mighty, majestic force of liberty ringing the jubilant sounds of revival fire for all to draw nigh to God and be set ablaze with pure truth from the heart of God.

Friend, you must allow God to do the fiery writing as you willfully listen and trust Him for all things good, holy, and pure to be deposited within your humble heart! The written and living Word wants to come alive in your heart every day! Say yes to Jesus and no to rebellion. The writing tablet of the heart receives the applications of God's Holy Word, where the applicable action is forming the divine nature of Jesus Christ within the humble heart!

> Forasmuch as ye are manifestly declared to be the epistle of Christ ministered by us, written not with ink, but with the Spirit of the living God; not in tables of stone, but in fleshy tables of the heart.
>
> 2 Corinthians 3:3 (KJV)

The Writing Tablet of a Selfless Heart

Psalm 45:1 (KJV), "My heart is inditing a good matter: I speak of the things which I have made touching the king: my tongue is the pen of a ready writer."

Friend, always allow your heart to be the writing tablet of heaven's truth, recording new life so you can enjoy a pure heart that will inherit heaven and be greatly rewarded for your own authenticity through Jesus Christ! Amen.

Friend, self must always get out of God's holy way, as He wants to take a heart and move it in the great blazing fire of heaven's momentum. As we gain momentum in Jesus Christ's Spirit-led ways, we lose all sense of self, meaning self-centeredness, selfish ambitions, and selfish pride.

Our selfless heart depicts the creative force of God as we thrive in its creative proof of His fiery anointing that manifests powerfully within our vessels daily.

Our heavenly Father is always fashioning, molding, and recording upon the tablets of hearts.

Millions around the world arise daily, making plans, filling schedules, and spending the day, if you will, in many carnal ways of self-indulgence and self-serving. How sad, as our heavenly Father is so grieved by the wayward ways of some of His creation, but He is waiting patiently for hearts to call upon Him in truth and humility day after day so He can write upon the tablet of their heart.

CHAPTER 12: HE MAKES FULL PROOF OF HIS ANOINTING ON YOU

Take Us, Lord!

Take us, Lord, into the anointed inner chamber of Your fiery heart, where the fire life of Your glorious radiance rests upon the sold-out vessel at the heights of eternity's covenant splendor that keeps us under Your majestic shadow only to overtake us with the fire of endless revival so we can powerfully impact the lives of souls with tangible demonstrations of Jesus Christ, the anointed one.

Salvation is a doorway to His kingdom. Taking up our cross and following Jesus daily is a lifestyle of living truth and proof of true religion and genuine Christianity! Amen.

> Then said Jesus unto them again, Verily, verily, I say unto you, I am the door of the sheep. All that ever came before me are thieves and robbers: but the sheep did not hear them. I am the door: by me if any man enter in, he shall be saved, and shall go in and out, and find pasture. The thief cometh not, but for to steal, and to kill, and to destroy: I am come that they might have life, and that they might have it more abundantly. I am the good shepherd: the good shepherd giveth his life for the sheep. But he

that is an hireling, and not the shepherd, whose own the sheep are not, seeth the wolf coming, and leaveth the sheep, and fleeth: and the wolf catcheth them, and scattereth the sheep. The hireling fleeth, because he is an hireling, and careth not for the sheep. I am the good shepherd, and know my sheep, and am known of mine. As the Father knoweth me, even so know I the Father: and I lay down my life for the sheep. And other sheep I have, which are not of this fold: them also I must bring, and they shall hear my voice; and there shall be one fold, and one shepherd. Therefore doth my Father love me, because I lay down my life, that I might take it again. No man taketh it from me, but I lay it down of myself. I have power to lay it down, and I have power to take it again. This commandment have I received of my Father. There was a division therefore again among the Jews for these sayings. And many of them said, He hath a devil, and is mad; why hear ye him?

John 10:7–20 (KJV)

Friend, Jesus Christ freely laid down His life for us because He wants to take us into His sheepfold and shepherd us and shield us in His glory, raising us in the strong anointing of heaven. Jesus also had the authority and power of His Father to take His life again. God has given us the choice to say back to Him, "Take us, Lord, and use us greatly for Your glory however You choose."

Our expressions and fellowship with the master are never accepted by the world, nor are they accepted by the spirit of religion. However, we were destined to move with the leading of the Holy Spirit in all faith, prayers, and humility. We do rise higher and greater in heaven's achievements because of the anointing that rests upon us! Friend, the operation and function of the anointing is a very serious lifestyle of total dependence and complete dedication to the Lord. We must never take it for granted because the anointing is the glorious power of the Father's heart that burns with the divine radiance of Jesus Christ within our humble vessels.

Friend, live life daily in the readiness of mind and heart harmonizing with the Holy Ghost being in the center of God's presence, speaking these pleasing words before the throne of grace, "Take me, Lord, for I wait and rest in You."

Remember, the repentant and pure heart will taste and know the kingdom identity realities in the revelations of the supernatural nature of God! His shining glory is your burning heart of supernatural reality stories! Living in the presence of God and His Word is real living that always takes the heart to the right place, and that is right before His holy face at the throne of intimate grace! The Word of the Lord is all proof and validating truth for all who stay within the salvation sheepfold of God's deliverance! Amen.

Take My Life

Take my life, make it whole, for I want to forever worship You in all holiness and all peace and all joy.

Take my life, for it is Yours. I lay it down in humility, and in all surrender, I give You all honor, all glory, and all praise.

Take my life, and bring me forth in the holy righteousness before Your face.

Take my life, and as You do, I will look only at You and follow You all my days.

Take my life, as I walk in reverential fear every day because I know You are always here, You are always with me, and You always show me in Your Holy Word how to live in holy fiery love and show it powerfully to the world.

Thank You for taking my life, for I don't want it in the hands of anything else other than the hands of a glorious, wonderful God!

He Makes Full Proof of His Anointing on You

Our heavenly Father's manifested presence makes full proof of His anointed truth on your life and also the demonstrations of His anointed authority in the golden glory realms of His holy power before the world and also before the powers of darkness.

When we abide in our destiny identity obedience to God our Holy Father, His Son, Jesus Christ, the Holy Spirit, we demonstrate as a flaming glory torch that carries the anointed Word of God deep within our surrendered vessel, thus impacting lives with a manifested substance that is God-breathed. God is pleased with you, child, when the ways of the world are placed behind you, and the kingdom of God's mandate is blazing with power within you as you take heaven's holy ways to peoples on the earth.

Friend, many years ago, the Lord spoke these profound words to me, "You don't have to prove who you are in Me, for My anointing upon your life will prove who you are in Me."

Note: substance in Hebrew means existence, essence, reality.

In the early years of walking in the anointing of God, He taught me how to allow the anointing to rest upon my vessel.

Rest in the mighty anointing of our wondrous living God! Rest well, drawing deeply from the master's well, for there is no drought in His eternal waters, nor is there any carnal dust in His living water.

His Endless River of the Anointing

Revelation 22:1 (KJV), "And he shewed me a pure river of water of life, clear as crystal, proceeding out of the throne of God and of the Lamb."

Revelation 22:17 (KJV), "And the Spirit and the bride say, Come. And let him that heareth say, Come. And let him that is athirst come. And whosoever will, let him take the water of life freely."

I had a powerful encounter with God. The setting was a very deep and mighty river; the waters were flowing very swiftly and very powerfully. The Lord spoke powerfully to me to jump into the river, and I obeyed. I wanted to swim, and the Lord spoke to me very powerfully not to swim, do no labor but flow in the anointing as the body of water was gently taking me at my free will and the rush of the force of flowing with glorious supernatural illumination. I knew I was in the river of God, and I did not work/labor to swim but I had full assurance that God and His anointing was the eternal flow in my heart and spirit as it would be for the rest of my life.

The river did not look like any river I'd ever seen in the natural world. The beauty in this encounter was the fact that the river was living and powerful, and I had to be 100 percent in submission mode and glorious rest, for the Lord wanted me to experience the powerful flow of the anointing in this supernatural life-enrichment encounter.

Friend, what a glorious and out-of-this-world experience. I was being spiritually submerged powerfully in the depths of spiritual wisdom and the glory flow of God's supreme authority. He is the Almighty forever and ever. The very flow of the anointing was like liquid fire and liquid glory; I felt like I was flowing in the living Word. The river was such life to my spirit that all I wanted to do was remain in the very holy and pure flow of my heavenly Father's heart and complete desires for every single heartbeat that He has allotted me upon the face of the earth thus far. You see, He lives in the face of the deep, but not with drowning power against His children but delivering power in the salvation mysteries to go deeper into His presence, His Word, and most of all, to be used for His glory. I remember as I was moving effortlessly in the river, God's Word was all through my vessel, and I knew it was all truth, all purity, and holiness flow of His majestic liquid glory.

Please note this encounter was about paying the price for the anointing. It was about living a consecrated life unto God. It was about living a life dedicated to the Word of God, the will of God, living in reverential fear that honors His holiness with the whole heart.

I was being used greatly in the anointing during this encounter, for it was my chosen mandate and destiny identity to flow in all my set-apart days as I totally surrendered to my king and His eternal splendor! I assure you I have paid a hefty price for this anointing that God has placed on my life. It has truly cost me everything! There is no way that I can fully explain the depth of my walk with the Lord in this book or in my daily life, as it is the same for all of you who are born again and walking with the *dunamis* and majestic God of the universe.

The Lord wants His children flowing in powerful anointing in these last days but *all* must pay their own price. Let us come alive in the anointing and move powerfully every hour that we can as time is coming to an end.

When someone first gets saved, they are born-again, but they are like a newborn baby in their salvation experience, and they must grow up. That takes time and self-discipline, adhering to the Word of God, and most of all, having a humble and contrite heart before the throne of grace. Just like babies in the nature, they don't grow up in a day—so is it in the supernatural; it takes time, process, and life experiences. God knows our spiritual journey growth process from beginning to end. I have experienced in these last days that many are acting as if they have grown up in a short span of time, but it takes time to gain wisdom. Many have knowledge of God and Christ's salvation; however, they lack wisdom and refuse to pay a high price for the anointing.

> Wherefore laying aside all malice, and all guile, and hypocrisies, and envies, and all evil speakings, As newborn babes, desire the sincere milk of the word, that ye may grow thereby: If so be ye have tasted that the Lord is gracious.
>
> 1 Peter 2:1–3 (KJV)

Babies always start out with a bottle before they can grow and develop more into solid foods, as it is in the walk with God and growing into the full age of spiritual maturity.

> And being made perfect, he became the author of eternal salvation unto all them that obey him; Called of God an high priest after the order of Melchisedec. Of whom we have many things to say, and hard to be uttered, seeing ye are dull of hearing. For when for the time ye ought to be teachers, ye have need that one teach you again which be the first principles of the oracles of God; and are become such as have need of milk, and not of strong meat. For every one that useth milk is unskilful in the word of righteousness: for he is a babe. But strong meat belongeth to them that are of full age, even those who by reason of use have their senses exercised to discern both good and evil.
>
> Hebrews 5:9–14 (KJV)

One must wholly desire maturity in the Holy Spirit with the eternal depths of truth, enlightening the way for the deeper submerging into the eternal flow of heaven's highest education in the supernatural life in Jesus Christ. We should never desire to stay as a babe in Christ because the enemy of darkness will bring a temptation of rebellion and disobedience that stifles the growth process, and in this occurrence, immaturity will crave entitlement, which stifles the spiritual vessel from receiving greater maturity in Jesus Christ. You see, at this carnal place, many will fall flat on their face because pride demands a self-serving agenda that refuses God's divine order of a profound growth process. Friend, obeying God is not a man-made agenda; it never has been, and it never will be! Don't be deceived; be delivered and be free today!

God knows all the levels of our understandings and He teaches all according to the daily dedication to the Lord.

Luke 8:10 (KJV), "And he said, Unto you it is given to know the mysteries of the kingdom of God: but to others in parables; that seeing they might not see, and hearing they might not understand."

Remember, the more one humbles before the master and obeys His Word, the faster the growth process. Amen!

The Fiery Tongue of Anointing Force

The baptism of the Holy Ghost, as recorded in Acts chapter 2, is the sustaining force of power that has been my way of life since 1983. The beautiful Holy Ghost prayer language (gift) bubbles up out of my vessel daily.

I know some Christians do not desire this holy gift. Paul said not all will speak in tongues. There are many gifts and offices for certain spiritual gifts.

Friend, praying in the Holy Ghost brings such powerful warfare strategies in the anointing, and the good Lord knew I needed this spiritual gift.

I personally had to have more for my very own life in the Spirit of Jesus Christ. This book is to help you reach your full potential in Jesus Christ so you can enter into the spiritual depths of the crucified life of Jesus Christ and also for a greater glory realm into His resurrection power.

Friend, if you desire and pray for the Acts 2 gifts and power, they are available for the born-again believers. It's a choice of yours.

I would encourage you to seek the Lord in child-like faith, having no fear of any recorded gifts in the Spirit, and allow Him to have His holy way in your heart and life, as the days are evil. We all need the greater works of Jesus to live in these perilous times.

The empowerment of the kingdom of God positions a heart to be endowed with glorious power in the baptism of the Holy Ghost, as recorded in Acts chapter 2, and wisdom in the throne room of holiness through total submission to the king of glory.

> In the last day, that great day of the feast, Jesus stood and cried, saying, If any man thirst, let him come unto me, and drink. He that believeth on me, as the scripture hath said, out of his belly shall flow rivers of living water. (But this spake he of the Spirit, which they that believe on him should receive: for the Holy Ghost was not yet given; because that Jesus was not yet glorified.)
>
> John 7:37–39 (KJV)

> Now ye are the body of Christ, and members in particular. And God hath set some in the church, first apostles, secondarily prophets, thirdly teachers, after that miracles, then gifts of healings, helps, governments, diversities of tongues. Are all apostles? are all prophets? are all teachers? are all workers of miracles? Have all the gifts of healing? do all speak with tongues? do all interpret? But covet earnestly the best gifts: and yet shew I unto you a more excellent way.
>
> 1 Corinthians 12:27–31 (KJV)

Friend, just remember these words of Jesus to His apostles, as recorded here in Acts chapter 1.

> The former treatise have I made, O Theophilus, of all that Jesus began both to do and teach, Until the day in which he was taken up, after that he through the Holy Ghost had given commandments unto the apostles

whom he had chosen: To whom also he shewed himself alive after his passion by many infallible proofs, being seen of them forty days, and speaking of the things pertaining to the kingdom of God: And, being assembled together with them, commanded them that they should not depart from Jerusalem, but wait for the promise of the Father, which, saith he, ye have heard of me. For John truly baptized with water; but ye shall be baptized with the Holy Ghost not many days hence. When they therefore were come together, they asked of him, saying, Lord, wilt thou at this time restore again the kingdom to Israel? And he said unto them, It is not for you to know the times or the seasons, which the Father hath put in his own power. But ye shall receive power, after that the Holy Ghost is come upon you: and ye shall be witnesses unto me both in Jerusalem, and in all Judaea, and in Samaria, and unto the uttermost part of the earth. And when he had spoken these things, while they beheld, he was taken up; and a cloud received him out of their sight.

Acts 1:1–9 (KJV)

The baptism of water is glorious; however, the baptism of fire in the Holy Ghost is supernatural in nature, which accelerates a heart into a glorious realm of divine fire and revival explosions that are beyond explanation. As I always say, you experience the Holy Spirit.

Friend, when one is praying in the beautiful Holy Ghost fire power, there is a union with fire of God in such a supernatural way as the Word is the tongue and the perfection of Jesus Christ is the burning flame of fire life in the spirit of divine communing as the Holy Spirit is a perfect balance in all kinds of prayers that truly surpasses our finite understandings. Still, in the infinite mind and Spirit of Jesus Christ, the highest anointed one, and the complete perfection of His Holy Father, there is a communication that only the Trinity can fully express in the perfect union of all wisdom.

We are taught mighty depths in our sacred prayer and intercession time with the Holy Spirit as we experience the perfect teachings in the Trinity.

Praying in the Holy Ghost is an honor of celestial proportions that is a sweet aroma before the throne of grace.

> But ye, beloved, building up yourselves on your most holy faith, praying in the Holy Ghost, Keep yourselves in the love of God, looking for the mercy of our Lord Jesus Christ unto eternal life. And of some have compassion, making a difference: And others save with fear, pulling them out of the fire; hating even the garment spotted by the flesh. Now unto him that is able to keep you from falling, and to present you faultless before the presence of his glory with exceeding joy, To the only wise God our Saviour, be glory and majesty, dominion and power, both now and ever. Amen.
>
> Jude 1:20–25 (KJV)

Friend, I say these words with an urgency within my heart, which is: Do not allow the devil to deceive you into thinking a little Word, a little prayer, and a little fellowship will reap a powerful life in the anointing depths of divine demonstrations of the kingdom of God.

I have taught the Word of God for many years and moved in a very strong anointing of God, and He gets all the glory, but I will also say this to all of you. Let me say that to whom much is given, much is required. Many people do not understand a crucified life in Jesus Christ and the very high cost for the glory realm of tangible manifestations in the anointing. Many want the power without paying the price. We must dedicate ourselves to much prayer.

> But he that knew not, and did commit things worthy of stripes, shall be beaten with few stripes. For unto whomsoever much is given, of him shall be much required: and to whom men have committed much, of him they will ask the more.
>
> Luke 12:48 (KJV)

The Lord told me that He required much of my life, but He also let me know that much suffering would be a huge part of my life. When God began to manifest powerfully in my life, I knew immediately that I was under hell's microscope. The greater revelation was that I was ever before the throne of grace and my heavenly Father's mighty delivering power for all my living breath and awakening days! Glory to God! All is well. Take that, powers of hell, in Jesus' name!

Friend, there is a jubilant force in the glory of God that sustains our sold-out vessel with great clarity and fortitude in the anointing of the Holy Ghost that hides our vessel in the Holy Ghost hideout of glory radiance protected in the hiding of the all-mighty power of God Himself!

Friend, rest assured, the more time you are with Him in the Word, prayer, and intimate fellowship, you will be more like Him, and the increase of the anointing will be upon your life powerfully!

In the sacred Scriptures, the Lord reminds us over and over how to love Him, know Him, and walk in resurrection power. In this very book, I am giving you many reminders to help you sojourn in your walk with the Lord so that you can learn well, go deeper into the heart of God, and receive powerfully from His multifaceted teachings. We go from glory to glory, and I pray you learn how to go from where you are now into the greater glory realm of truth and supernatural experiences that are pure and holy straight from the heart of God to your child-like faith-filled heart.

God can do anything He wants to; just believe that He wants to demonstrate powerfully through you. The devil hates the anointing…so what? He's crushed under your anointed feet!

God loves to take us in the powerful direction of His Word reflections where our hearts are ever flooded with His holy wisdom and greater character building in the solid foundation of pure truth to the end of our days! Amen!

> A prayer of Habakkuk the prophet upon Shigionoth. O Lord, I have heard thy speech, and was afraid: O Lord, revive thy work in the midst of the years, in the midst of the years make known; in wrath remember mercy. God came from Teman, and the Holy One from mount Paran. Selah. His glory covered the heavens, and the earth was full of his praise. And his brightness was as the light; he had horns coming out of his hand: and there was the hiding of his power. Before him went the pestilence, and burning coals went forth at his feet. He stood, and measured the earth: he beheld, and drove asunder the nations; and the everlasting mountains were scattered, the perpetual hills did bow: his ways are everlasting.
>
> Habakkuk 3:1–6 (KJV)

Many years ago, I went through some horrific warfare, and I told God that He had all but let me go through a living hell for this anointing that I carry in my vessel. He said, "It is to bring heaven to the hearts here below. I have a deep love for souls, but some don't have a love for Me at all, as was for Jesus Christ!"

I will serve him through His Word and the fire of His anointing until my last day in His universe! No matter what comes my way, I am here to stay until He calls me away. Take that, devil. In Jesus' name!

Come Forth in Your Anointing, Son and Daughter of Destiny

How do you know when to step out in the anointing?

How do you know your own name? You just know it. You just know it through the power of Jesus Christ that rests upon you.

If you truly do what is required of you in the Holy Word, then your set time has arrived.

Remember, don't make the plans of God complicated concerning your life as God teaches all His children in the simplicity of Jesus Christ with all power and all authority with the wisdom of heaven ruling the saved, sold-out heart.

Our Christian journey with Jesus Christ in the fire of His anointing should always be kept in the simple heart action of a powerful and deep prayer life in every twenty-four-seven cycle of time that unfolds before us. How many out there know that spending time with *God in prayer is a powerful and fruitful lifestyle* that becomes more enriched as the days unfold?

Prayer is a supernatural action of the heart that needs no explanation. The Holy Spirit is the fire force of our rich prayer resource in our quest for heaven, which is a powerful spiritual explosion in the spiritual conquest in the earth against the forces of evil.

A deep prayer and Word life manifest a deep knowledge and revelation in the power of Jesus Christ, and Word accelerations of kingdom wisdom attributes advancing the heart into the inner chamber of the heavenly Father's holy heart of beautiful glory, wonders, and miraculous rewards.

Jesus Christ, the Anointed One, Is the Great Intercessor

Oh, how sweet it is when you realize that Jesus is praying for you and wanting the best for you in this world today. Allow the Lord to show you His love and receive His intercessory prayers for your life! He is the most powerful and faithful intercessor without imperfection and flaws. He is forever seated at the right hand of power with you on His mind!

Romans 8:34 (KJV), "Who is he that condemneth? It is Christ that died, yea rather, that is risen again, who is even at the right hand of God, who also maketh intercession for us."

Friend, Jesus Christ loves to pray for you. He is seated high upon His throne in heaven, and He is non-stop interceding for souls in the earth, and that is glorious and joyous news to think someone is praying for you. Jesus Christ is supernatural, and He always has humanity on His mind and in His heart before His Holy Father.

I have heard different people say for many years that God is too busy with other important things for Him to be thinking of them too much, or Jesus praying for them, as He has so many to pray for! Friend, those words are from a heart filled with unbelief and lack of knowledge. Let me say these words in this chapter: Jesus is never too busy to pray for you. You are deeply loved and cared for by Him, and He is seated at the right hand of God, where He is praying for you daily. Don't allow unbelief to govern your heart and mind, as it is not the truth of God. Call upon God today to help you in every way.

Hebrews 7:25 (KJV), "Wherefore he is able also to save them to the uttermost that come unto God by him, seeing he ever liveth to make intercession for them."

Jesus Christ wants to save all lost hearts, as it is not His will that any perish and be lost without the salvation in Him. It's a beautiful and wonderful thought knowing that Jesus loves you so deeply, and no matter how dark and evil your present life is or what you have done, He is here for you now to save you, set you free, set you on fire for His intimate glory, and place you in a high place of holiness and godliness, where your heart will be a perpetual flame of glory fire life in the holiness of heaven in all liberation and joyous celebrations!

Matthew 5:44 (KJV), "But I say unto you, Love your enemies, bless them that curse you, do good to them that hate you, and pray for them which despitefully use you, and persecute you."

The Lord showed me an open vision of the sky above me, these words as they were written in the clouds: *love your enemies*. What a way of a required life for me, and doing just that, my whole Christian walk has been trying, but with divine intervention and my deep love for God, I have obeyed and interceded for all of them. You will always have enemies on the earth, but you can press on in the powerful anointing of God and grow in greater wisdom as the maturity of God increases in your humble and sold-out heart. Praying for others is a humble experience that captivates and elevates the heart in the perfect will of God. Jesus prays for His enemies. Remember, Jesus prayed this prayer on the cross, and we can pray it, too. Amen.

Luke 23:34 (KJV), "Then said Jesus, Father, forgive them; for they know not what they do. And they parted his raiment, and cast lots."

Friend, when we pray for others, self is out of the forefront of the heart and mind, and that is pleasing to God. We must fast at times for souls; it is imperative to put others always before self! Amen.

A Powerful Plan of God for Fasting

> Is not this the fast that I have chosen? to loose the bands of wickedness, to undo the heavy burdens, and to let the oppressed go free, and that ye break every yoke? Is it not to deal thy bread to the hungry, and that thou bring the poor that are cast out to thy house? when thou seest

the naked, that thou cover him; and that thou hide not thyself from thine own flesh? Then shall thy light break forth as the morning, and thine health shall spring forth speedily: and thy righteousness shall go before thee; the glory of the Lord shall be thy reward. Then shalt thou call, and the Lord shall answer; thou shalt cry, and he shall say, Here I am. If thou take away from the midst of thee the yoke, the putting forth of the finger, and speaking vanity; And if thou draw out thy soul to the hungry, and satisfy the afflicted soul; then shall thy light rise in obscurity, and thy darkness be as the noon day: And the Lord shall guide thee continually, and satisfy thy soul in drought, and make fat thy bones: and thou shalt be like a watered garden, and like a spring of water, whose waters fail not. And they that shall be of thee shall build the old waste places: thou shalt raise up the foundations of many generations; and thou shalt be called, The repairer of the breach, The restorer of paths to dwell in. If thou turn away thy foot from the sabbath, from doing thy pleasure on my holy day; and call the sabbath a delight, the holy of the Lord, honourable; and shalt honour him, not doing thine own ways, nor finding thine own pleasure, nor speaking thine own words: Then shalt thou delight thyself in the Lord; and I will cause thee to ride upon the high places of the earth, and feed thee with the heritage of Jacob thy father: for the mouth of the Lord hath spoken it.

Isaiah 58:6–14 (KJV)

Prayer and Fasting

Friend, walking in a powerful anointing, there are times that we must pray and fast for one's deliverance. We can never rebuke a devil with unbelief in our hearts. We have authority over the powers of darkness. We must exercise it before all demons and people.

In wisdom, of course.

Fasting is an honor to deny one of self, humble the heart before God, and intercede on behalf of others to see a powerful breakthrough and deliverance of total transformation. I would encourage you today to study prayer and fasting, rising in the love for souls, and accomplish mighty things in the heart action of prayer and fasting without announcing every detail on the housetops. Like I always say, sometimes you get more accomplished in intercessory prayer in the spirit without announcing it to the world. In fasting, there are deliverances, healings, and restorations—major things transpire in fasting.

> And Jesus rebuked the devil; and he departed out of him: and the child was cured from that very hour. Then came the disciples to Jesus apart, and said, Why could not we cast him out? And Jesus said unto them, Because of your unbelief: for verily I say unto you, If ye have faith as a grain of mustard seed, ye shall say unto this mountain, Remove hence to yonder place; and it shall remove; and nothing shall be impossible unto you. Howbeit this kind goeth not out but by prayer and fasting.
>
> Matthew 17:18–21 (KJV)

CHAPTER 13: A GOD-GIVEN, ANOINTED DREAM

His Untouched Anointed Dream within You

Friend, I want to share with you in this chapter some experiences that I went through that may help you, warn you, but also expose the works of darkness that will manifest before your face, and perhaps you have already had these wicked works come against you as well. As I am writing this book, I am so reminded of the hostile warfare that I have endured for the gospel's sake, and I know many of you out there are feeling the same in your anointed vessels as well.

God didn't throw away your dream, so don't you throw it away, for it will come to fruition in God's perfect timing! Only believe. What God has placed within your sold-out vessel, no one else on Earth can have it! It is set apart just for you alone, as the anointing is solely upon you to carry the glory fire that is from God to you! You have paid the high price for the *Holy Ghost kingdom merchandise*; no one else paid the price for your salvation and the anointing, only Jesus Christ Himself. Period! Amen!

When God has given you a dream, it has been given to you and no one else. Nobody can steal your dream; that is God's holy dream within your vessel! You have been chosen, and you know it, and all of Heaven will back you up and defeat all the workings of evil against the anointing on your life and the anointed dreams and gifts that are set apart just for you! Amen! Take that, devil, in Jesus' name!

Rest assured, God will demonstrate powerfully through authenticity, and He will faithfully expose the counterfeit! No fraud will receive heaven's applause.

God gave an anointed dream to Joseph, not to his brothers. Amen.

The anointing was upon Joseph to fulfill the dream that God placed within his heart. There was simply no other human on Earth that could fulfill the destiny that Joseph was created for, and it is the same for you in your faithful walk with God.

Friend, isn't that lovely news?

> Now Israel loved Joseph more than all his children, because he was the son of his old age: and he made him a coat of many colours. And when his brethren saw that their father loved him more than all his brethren, they hated him, and could not speak peaceably unto him. And Joseph dreamed a dream, and he told it his brethren: and they hated him yet the more. And he said unto them, Hear, I pray you, this dream which I have dreamed: For, behold, we were binding sheaves in the field, and, lo, my sheaf arose, and also stood upright; and, behold, your sheaves stood round about, and made obeisance to my sheaf. And his brethren said to him, Shalt thou indeed reign over us? or shalt thou indeed have dominion over us? And they hated him yet the more for his dreams, and for his words. And he dreamed yet another dream, and told it his brethren, and said, Behold, I have dreamed a dream more; and, behold, the sun and the moon and the eleven stars made obeisance to me. And he told it to his father, and to his brethren: and his father rebuked him, and said unto him, What is this dream that thou hast dreamed? Shall I and thy mother and thy brethren indeed come to bow down ourselves to thee to the earth? And his brethren envied

him; but his father observed the saying.

Genesis 37:3–11 (KJV)

Joseph wore a coat of many colors, but I call it a coat of many troubles because of the great sufferings that he would experience due to the kingdom dream that he carried in His humble vessel!

March on, Dreamer

Genesis 37:19 (KJV), "And they said one to another, Behold, this dreamer cometh."

Friend, I had prayed and asked God to retire from my flight attendant position for years so I could move to Kentucky and go full-time ministry, which was a God-given dream within my heart. I so wanted to be in the center of the harvest field, encouraging souls to become saved with the revival fire blazing deep within my heart, taking the gospel to souls as God directed, also exhorting others to do likewise as time is getting closer to Jesus Christ's return.

In one single day, while I was walking through my home, the Lord visited me in a mighty way. I fell on my knees in my old Victorian home in Coldwater, Michigan, where I was greatly humbled before God in reverential fear to the point that I was trembling in His glorious presence. He then began speaking to me about profound things. He showed me a huge male figure in a powerful masculine form walking through cities in our nation, destroying idols that had been set up by humans. He said he had had it with the idolatry in our nation and around the world. He told me that there would be many deaths in 2020 and that souls must get right before Him. He spoke to me about other things that I am not permitted to disclose at this given time.

He told me to retire from the airline and move to Kentucky. I was engulfed in the very glory of Almighty God. I will tell you this:

God wants hearts to get saved and become sold out for the gospel's sake and also for reverential fear to fall upon all hearts on the earth. God is a serious God and holy, and oh how He loves people. He wants the church to become holy and prepared for His soon return. It's a kingdom mandate for souls to repent and wholeheartedly serve God and point the lost to the king of glory. Remember, true love is telling the pure truth of God's written Word.

Friend, I was carrying a beautiful dream within my heart for many decades and that dream was to write a book. I shared it with some people that I thought loved me, only to find out that swine were in my midst, and the wicked ways of jealousy began to manifest through their superficial behaviors and other wicked works against the anointing and dreams that God had placed within my heart. The devil always goes after the anointing! He hates what we authentically possess in Jesus Christ.

Many are called, but few are chosen.

Friend, if one is really saved, they will have a pure heart and pure motives, they will be washed clean by the blood of the lamb, their wedding garment will be spotless, and their heart will be ready to be with their heavenly bridegroom and daily walking in the attributes of His holiness. Amen.

> Then saith he to his servants, The wedding is ready, but they which were bidden were not worthy. Go ye therefore into the highways, and as many as ye shall find, bid to the marriage. So those servants went out into the highways, and gathered together all as many as they found, both bad and good: and the wedding was furnished with guests. And when the king came in to see the guests, he saw there a man which had not on a wedding garment: And he saith unto him, Friend, how camest thou in hither not having a wedding garment? And he was speechless. Then said the king to the servants, Bind him hand and

foot, and take him away, and cast him into outer darkness, there shall be weeping and gnashing of teeth. For many are called, but few are chosen.

Matthew 22:8–14 (KJV)

Friend, you know you are chosen because the chosen stay sold out, set apart, and walking in truth, holiness, and righteousness. You will always desire to please God and abstain from the evil works of darkness. You will always want to remain in the light of truth for the rest of your living days. You can do it in Jesus' name! When the fire of God burns in a sold-out heart, nothing can kill you off the earth, no matter the onslaughts the enemies of darkness throw your anointed way. The Lord gave me this word years ago: The devil attacks the flesh, but he cannot have your spirit nor destroy it!

Ephesians 1:4 (KJV), "According as he hath chosen us in him before the foundation of the world, that we should be holy and without blame before him in love."

The enemy wanted my dream destroyed on all levels. God will never permit evil to prevail against your life, for He will always expose the plots and deal with all that have been pawns of the enemy through jealousy, envy, and all other evil invasions against God's anointing on your life!

Friend, no devil or human can destroy the plan that God has just for you, so don't be blue, for God will make your dreams come true!

Spiritual Identity Theft

Friend, sadly, there are some people out there who think they are entitled to the anointing, the gifts, and the dreams that God has placed on your life! What lies and wickedness have blinded those people who think they can steal one's spiritual identity?

My spiritual identity belongs to God, and no devil or any other human can have it. It is not for sale. It is out of this world because it is *not* of this world. I cannot fully explain myself, but God completely knows me. We are not of this world, so let us come up higher in our understanding of why the devil always wants our spiritual identity.

No one can have who you fully are in Jesus Christ. He died to reveal who you are. As I always say, Jesus Christ has given us a treasure trove of kingdom identity understanding recorded in Scriptures. In Christ, we are His living destiny, fashioned in His identity attributes and living in the wealth of His identity fulfillment and destiny pleasures.

People need to experience their own identity in Christ. Amen!

People will never fully understand your life. It's not about them understanding you; it's all about you fully obeying God.

Tell the devil your identity is not for sale, and he can't touch it in the name of Jesus.

It's so glorious being the original you before the throne of grace.

Some people need to get over their prideful, entitled selves and move into the refinement furnace of purification and accountability, where repentance before God rules the heart instead of thievery, jealousy, and envy.

Those who covet what you have don't know God intimately or His covenant, period.

Friend, beware of superficial relationships. I have had the privilege of meeting many people in my life, and I'm so thankful to have been able to have them cross my path. I had some come into my life years ago that ended up being fair-weathered friends, only surface relationships that turned out for me to be very toxic and demonic, to say the least. Some people will only use you for their own selfish ambitions and ill-gotten gains, and those kinds of people's behaviors have no real foundation of authenticity and pure motives! Woe, woe be to those who plot evil against the Lord's anointed.

Psalm 101:7 (KJV), "He that worketh deceit shall not dwell within my house: he that telleth lies shall not tarry in my sight."

Song of Solomon 8:6 (KJV), "Set me as a seal upon thine heart, as a seal upon thine arm: for love is strong as death; jealousy is cruel as the grave: the coals thereof are coals of fire, which hath a most vehement flame."

Friend, never allow jealousy to invade your heart and spirit, as it is the working of the devil; it will, without fail, utterly destroy relationships every time. It is set on fire from hell, and it will consume a heart, leaving it to bitter self-destruction and open shame before God. Always love with a pure heart and pure motives, but some hearts will never be pure toward another. Some people want what you have, but they don't want you. Amen!

God warned me in a dream of a betrayal. The more that God promoted me in ministry, the more wicked jealousy began to manifest, and later, a greater injustice was done against my life and the anointing that God placed upon me. Spiritual identity theft happens every day, as some people think they are entitled to have *all* that God has placed in your vessel. Not so! They are gravely deceived by the devil! Take note: The devil is not entitled to have the anointing on your life, and no other human is entitled to have it, either. We have our own unique authenticity in Jesus Christ as born-again believers.

Friend, this is the very nature of Lucifer.

Spiritual identity theft in the natural realm ends in a prison sentence due to such a ruthless criminal act. Spiritual identity theft in the spirit realm is a criminal act as well. It is the very nature of Lucifer himself as he wanted God's identity, and God is Spirit! Amen.

> How art thou fallen from heaven, O Lucifer, son of the morning! how art thou cut down to the ground, which

didst weaken the nations! For thou hast said in thine heart, I will ascend into heaven, I will exalt my throne above the stars of God: I will sit also upon the mount of the congregation, in the sides of the north: I will ascend above the heights of the clouds; I will be like the most High. Yet thou shalt be brought down to hell, to the sides of the pit. They that see thee shall narrowly look upon thee, and consider thee, saying, Is this the man that made the earth to tremble, that did shake kingdoms; That made the world as a wilderness, and destroyed the cities thereof; that opened not the house of his prisoners?

Isaiah 14:12–17 (KJV)

Friend, Lucifer wanted God's throne and His spiritual identity, but that was not possible. God Almighty is supreme, and nothing can move Him from His everlasting governing and authoritative position. Nothing above the earth, on the earth, or under the earth can have God's identity or yours! No one can have your fingerprint or God's master blueprint for your anointed life! Take that, devil! In Jesus' name!

There is a word that is widely used these days; it's "narcissism." That's the world's terminology, but God and Jesus Christ and the Holy Spirit call it "demons, demons, demons," as they are rapidly invading the earth, and *many* people need *deliverance*. The Holy Ghost's fire power needs to be the heart of the end-time church and put all these lying devils to flight in Jesus' mighty name!

Jesus Christ had zero tolerance concerning demons in His day, and the good Lord knows there is more demonic activity in our day. Still, much of the church has become so weak that they entertain devils daily, as some are handing their children over to them in many carnal ways.

When this invasion of spiritual identity theft came against my life in Jesus Christ, which has been more than once, every time it has occurred, God gave me these powerful scriptures to stand on, and I'm so thrilled that His Word cannot lie.

Psalm 105:15 (KJV), "Saying, Touch not mine anointed, and do my prophets no harm."

Deuteronomy 32:10 (KJV), "He found him in a desert land, and in the waste howling wilderness; he led him about, he instructed him, he kept him as the apple of his eye."

Romans 12:19 (KJV), "Dearly beloved, avenge not yourselves, but rather give place unto wrath: for it is written, Vengeance is mine; I will repay, saith the Lord."

Matthew 18:21–22 (KJV),

> Then came Peter to him, and said, Lord, how oft shall my brother sin against me, and I forgive him? till seven times? Jesus saith unto him, I say not unto thee, Until seven times: but, Until seventy times seven.

And also the entire chapter of Psalm 35.

God has given me more scriptures, but these are the ones I want to share with you.

Friend, when someone commits spiritual identity theft, they are deceived by the devil and take on the nature of hell by living an all-out lie because they want something so bad that does not rightfully belong to them, so they will do just about anything to obtain a fake and false identity. The truth is, they do not have their own identity in spirit and truth. They identify with the powers of darkness and produce the greater wages of sin upon their own lives, heaping up more self-destruction and carnal captivity. There is absolutely no reverential fear of God in this type of behavior. Note: See Romans 6:23.

I have forgiven much in my life, for I always say I will not go to hell for unforgiveness and bitterness. Let me say this with an urgency in my spirit: Some people will go to hell for unrepentant sin, and if they live a lie and die in the lie, there is no escaping the eternal sentence in hell.

I only pray that all will repent and turn away from these wicked sins and allow God to reign righteousness within the heart. That way, freedom can show the straight way of working out one's own salvation with fear and trembling and do their own set apart work in Jesus as He has planned for them in their authentic identity formed in Jesus Christ-likeness and His kingdom attributes.

The truth is much of the world is in an identity crisis, but as bornagain Christians, we are to be in kingdom destiny identity and covenant accountability realities with our living and breathing and teaching Word, Jesus Christ Himself. To know kingdom identity realities in Jesus Christ is truly living an abundant life and wealthy success in the Godhead. Nothing less than that, my friend, should ever be accepted within your spirit but only rebuked and cast down and cast out of your vessel and presence. Amen! Note: 3 John 2.

Remember, the devil seeks to devour. Refuse to allow him to devour any part of your life because he is a devourer of grave destruction and torment who wants all souls in eternal damnation with him forever and ever.

Familiar Friend

A familiar friend is not a faithful and true friend. They will always be as Judas in your midst, consumed with the wickedness of hell, being determined to destroy your life and all that you stand for in the very anointing of God. In fact, God spoke to me these profound words and I pray they encourage you: They will sacrifice you to build their own self-made kingdom. This sounds familiar, doesn't it? Jesus Christ knows this all too well. A man-made kingdom always falls into utter destruction and complete exposure due to all the carnal works of the flesh and its fallen nature to crave the wickedness of Satan.

God is the master builder of the heart. He builds His anointed and chosen ones on the foundation of truth and the greater works of Jesus Christ, His Son, so that the beauty of our temple is the very Holy Spirit and the depositing of His kingdom treasures are untouched by the world. The very exquisite display of them is in all holiness, righteousness, purity, and genuineness.

A self-made kingdom is built on carnal sand, and it will always be destroyed because there is only one foundation that is able to stand before God. It's the solid rock foundation of truth, which is Jesus Christ's divine nature of faithful promises that are without carnal dust of this world and marred flaws!

> Yea, mine own familiar friend, in whom I trusted, which did eat of my bread, hath lifted up his heel against me. But thou, O Lord, be merciful unto me, and raise me up, that I may requite them. By this I know that thou favourest me, because mine enemy doth not triumph over me. And as for me, thou upholdest me in mine integrity, and settest me before thy face for ever. Blessed be the Lord God of Israel from everlasting, and to everlasting. Amen, and Amen.
>
> Psalm 41:9–13 (KJV)

Rejoice, friend, and press on in the battle; far greater things come to a pure heart with pure motives! You always have the victory! Amen.

God spoke this to me many years ago, "The greater the battle, the greater the victory. The greater the onslaught, the greater the anointing."

Genesis 50:20 (KJV), "But as for you, ye thought evil against me; but God meant it unto good, to bring to pass, as it is this day, to save much people alive."

When God turns all for your good, He gives back far more than you could ever begin to imagine! Amen!

A True and Genuine Friend

God wants total lordship over all our friendships.

Proverbs 27:17 (KJV), "Iron sharpeneth iron; so a man sharpeneth the countenance of his friend."

God has truly blessed me with true friends. What a rare jewel to have wholesome relationships with friends who genuinely love you without any kind of ulterior motive. They know the unity of brethren that shines upon friendships and carries the union into greater depths of truth and peace before God.

True and lasting friendships should harmonize with the authenticity of heaven's blessings, thus being a loving example filled with truth and healthy influence in the Spirit of God.

Friend, a true friend loves you and will always tell you the truth, whether you want to hear it or not, because truth brings liberation, not bondage, to the enslavements of sin. True friends are never jealous or envious, but they celebrate all the successes in your life, and they are genuinely happy for you. This is the divine plan of God for pure relationships on the earth.

The Friendship of David and Jonathan

King Saul was so jealous and envious of David and wanted him dead. However, Saul's son, Jonathan, loved David as His own soul, being that he loved him with a pure and wholesome love. He helped David because Saul was afraid of David, as God had rejected Saul as king, and David was anointed to be the king over all of Israel. See 1 Samuel 16:1–13.

Jonathan cared about David's well-being because he knew very well that his father was out to destroy the Lord's anointed, but God would never allow David to be destroyed by the hand of Saul. Jonathan wanted David to have his robe, his garments, his sword, his bow, and his girdle.

The love of Jonathan and David was first from above, and all friendships on Earth should be as they were, as far as love and mutual respect. It's only sad to say, but few really experience this type of friendship. The world and some in the church are truly getting farther and farther away from the one true living God and His guiding principles of truth for daily living. God help us.

> And it came to pass, when he had made an end of speaking unto Saul, that the soul of Jonathan was knit with the soul of David, and Jonathan loved him as his own soul. And Saul took him that day, and would let him go no more home to his father's house. Then Jonathan and David made a covenant, because he loved him as his own soul. And Jonathan stripped himself of the robe that was upon him, and gave it to David, and his garments, even to his sword, and to his bow, and to his girdle.
>
> 1 Samuel 18:1–4 (KJV)

Don't Cast Your Kingdom Pearls before Swine

Matthew 7:6 (KJV), "Give not that which is holy unto the dogs, neither cast ye your pearls before swine, lest they trample them under their feet, and turn again and rend you."

I love teaching the Word of God to souls, as ministry is my heart's desire. To encourage souls to reach their full potential in God is a mandate from heaven for me. However, I have encountered some people who are used by the devil against my life due to deep-rooted envy and jealousy that have consumed their hearts against the anointing of my life. Friend, some people do not want you to succeed, nor do they celebrate your successes.

My mother taught me well even from a young age; she would always tell me to be happy for other people when God blesses their lives and when good things come their way, whether in finances or achievements. I praise God that I, too, do the same, and I taught my son as I was taught. It is so important to be happy and enjoy the things that come down from the Father of lights to souls! I am so grieved when I see some people be so fueled by hell because their hearts are so filled with jealousy against another human being. The days are evil, and we are seeing so much of the works of the flesh, even in some Christians. It is hard to witness this type of behavior in my midst because you can never build strong relationships with these types of people because they become an enemy in your face.

I remember times in my younger years when God would reveal spiritual things to me, and my heart wanted others to know of these things so they could be deeply encouraged and grow closer to God. Sometimes, it didn't work that way; more often than not, jealousy, envy, and mocking would manifest within their hearts and pull away from me because of the spiritual walk I have with the Lord. I wanted souls to go deeper into the Spirit with God and not limit Him, but almost always, unbelief started trampling the pearl. My overall experience in sharing my testimony and the depths of God's supernatural experiences was more accepted by the lost souls than by some of my Christian brothers and sisters. The body of Christ needs to be fully immersed in the lifestyle of Christ's righteous ways so we can collectively and corporately be unified in the love of Jesus Christ and destroy the works of Satan instead of being combative and working against those in the household of faith!

I have learned not to say certain things and remain silent until the

Lord releases me to share with some people. Sometimes, it's best to hold your words and keep them to yourself, as there are some that scoff and mock your pure words that are sent down from God above through your surrendered vessel. Pray for the souls and keep moving on to the greater things of God.

Friend, you will always have people come against the anointing on your life. Rest in trust and watch the goodness of God in your life because we want souls going to heaven and not hell. Repentance is a glorious thing. It will allow God to transform a heart so He can use it powerfully before the peoples on the earth.

Your Inner Circle

Friend, we must use wisdom as to who abides in our inner circle, for it is vitally important in these last days. I had allowed some people to get close to me who had no desire to be genuine before me but wanted harm on all levels to hit my life, and God had warned me about certain things concerning them and what was to come forth. I sought the Lord on their behalf but to no avail due to their toxic heart condition of rebellion against God and His servant. I knew that God was going to deal with the situation, and He did.

I would love to write in these pages that everything is wonderful in the world, in our lives, and in the church. Stop.... Reality check with Scripture references.

There is a reason Paul wrote this scripture, "If it be possible, as much as lieth in you, live peaceably with all men" (Romans 12:18, KJV). Some didn't want to live in peace with Paul. That is the way of the world; they don't want God, His Word, and a holy lifestyle. Paul kept preaching, he kept writing, and he kept demonstrating the power and authority of Jesus Christ!

Many didn't want to live in peace with Jesus Christ, but rather, they wanted Him killed.

We must strive to do the best that we can, serving the Lord with a pure heart and pure motives. Amen!

Friend, your inner circle of people should always be with people who are serious about God and the saving of souls and want to see the demons defeated. I don't know about you, but I've had my share of Job's friends. All the friends that have come into my life are for the purpose of spiritual education and greater maturity in the context that people's behavior, at times, can be very challenging. However, we must never forget that Jesus Christ knows from beginning to end how our relationships will turn out as our life experiences unfold, whether they are good or major disruptions that are toxic and unhealthy for us. God is always faithful to show us how to handle all relationships as we faithfully seek His face for wisdom in all human interactions. Rest assured; you will learn the seasons of relationships.

Job 42:10 (KJV), "And the Lord turned the captivity of Job, when he prayed for his friends: also the Lord gave Job twice as much as he had before."

The Lord began to speak to me years ago about guarding my inner circle of friends because there was spiritual warfare taking place. One day, while I was seeking His face, He spoke these words to me, "I shall fan away from thee all of the wrong friends, for they shall be as chaff blowing in the wind, and I shall place around thee those that are pure in heart toward thee."

God has truly been faithful in doing just that. Later, He took me to this very scripture. I have held onto it since the word came forth.

> Let them be confounded and put to shame that seek after my soul: let them be turned back and brought to confusion that devise my hurt. Let them be as chaff before the wind: and let the angel of the Lord chase them.
>
> Psalm 35:4–5 (KJV)

Friend, loving people is God's perfect will and plan for our lives. I have practiced this word for many, many years, and I have found such liberty and productivity in the beauty of these revealing words that the Lord spoke to me: Release and increase, and I do just that. When you have done everything within you to invest in other lives and serve them with the attributes of Jesus Christ that faithfully flow through your anointed vessel, but they choose to be opposite of the ways of God and His delivering Word, pray for God to give you direction. It might be that the season for that friendship has ended, and as you pray for them and release them at the feet of Jesus, you must keep doing as God has commissioned you to do. I have always experienced an increase in my walk with God when I learn to let go and move forward in the anointed kingdom work that rests within my vessel. We pray for all souls, but we must always remember that God knows best how to deal with every human on the planet. He is in full control, not us. Amen!

I pray this helps you as I share what I do in all friendship relationships in my presence.

I invest in their lives with all that is within me.

I love with the love of God.

I pray and intercede for souls.

I encourage all to the highest in Jesus Christ, our Lord.

I trust God in all things pertaining to the relationship.

I pay close attention to the gift of discernment.

When the time comes to release and let go, I must obey God and trust Him for the outcome.

Remember, you are not the Savior; therefore, it is best to move completely out of God's way, as He wants full reign over all things pertaining to our lives and relationships.

Friend, may I share with you this word of wisdom: Don't hold onto something that God has already moved out of your life. There will always be many people with opinions that stir around. Still, our decisions should never be based on the opinions of others but the hearkening to the Word of the Lord in all the observations of daily abiding in the covenant fellowship with the perfect and faithful all-time best friend, Jesus Christ our Lord.

In my own personal life, I fully go with the leading of the Holy Spirit and not the opinions of outside sources. Many people mean well; however, we cannot be led by the flesh under any circumstance. If you notice, there will be all kinds of people who think they know what is best for you, but the truth is God knows what is best for all of humanity. However, many never seek His guidance or trust His power to lead. Many are still in great bondage to pride and its arrogant demands of control, thus having no self-control themselves.

I have had to learn from my own mistakes in the past when someone thought they knew the direction of the ministry for my life, and I had a check in my spirit that was not the leading of the Holy Spirit. I had to repent before God for making this mistake that was never my master's plan, period. He watched out for me, as He always does. God is so faithful!

Friend, I was created to go to peoples around the globe and share the gospel with hearts, so whether people receive my anointing or not, it's okay because God is always looking for and rewarding a humble heart that is tried and true and seeks to live in obedience. The opinions of others don't move me; only the covenant commands of God burn powerfully within me.

Friend, we should always want what God wants for our lives and not what we think He wants for our lives. There should always be a peaceful knowing within our hearts and not a fleshly assumption of being caught off guard and becoming the fallen prey to toxic and unhealthy relationships that wage a battle against the anointing daily.

The people in our inner circle should be intercessors for us, as we likewise should do for them. Remember, the inner circle always touches the inner core of your being. That's why your inner circle is deeply important and why the sphere of influence is all-encompassed of God's perfect plans and harmonious in all fellowship to be like-minded and one in Jesus Christ. Friend, your inner circle is very important to God, and it should be held up in the holy accountability of truth, divine unity, and the bonds of peace before the throne of God.

We all need prayer because there is such hostile spiritual warfare taking place on the earth every day. Learn to guard your inner circle with rich wisdom and discernment. It is imperative to cover all relationships with prayer because the enemy will always come around to attack every single friendship in your life. Take note of it. Hell's assignment is ultimate destruction.

Remember, light and darkness have no fellowship. There are other people in the earth that God wants us to invest in; therefore, we must allow ourselves to enter all the new seasons that are before us with alertness and willingness to embrace all new assignments and graciously walk on.

CHAPTER 14: PREACH THE GOSPEL IN THE RADIANT FORCE OF GLORY FIRE

Chosen Ministries Choosing the Fullness of Jesus Christ

Greetings to all ministers globally,

Friend, I write this to you with a fiery urgency within my heart, burning in the royal flames of heaven. Oh holy fire, burn, burn and touch every minister near and far and stir their vessel with the refiner's fire of flaming glory and holy accountability to the point where nothing is left but the perpetual flaming truth of heaven's validating proof of holiness and righteousness being the revival mandate for all ministers and ministries worldwide. Jesus Christ, the anointed one in you, yearns to demonstrate great power and authority through your humble vessel, also with greater conviction for the global vision to see souls saved, set free, and miracles taking place on a much greater scale that the world has never witnessed before.

The world is in great turmoil and suffering, which is why it is imperative to heed the master's glory call to wholehearted submission and carry out your powerful mission with the burning desire to sound a worldwide wake-up call to all by waving the victory banner on high with shouts of praise. The hour has come for all to bow before the throne of grace in true repentance and make a righteous stand for truth and freedom in Jesus Christ, no matter the cost. The devil is pushing to influence hearts to a confused identity and also a lukewarm gospel. The devil is setting the stage for the anti-Christ appearance, as he is everything (anti-Christ nature), and he wants to destroy God's holy identity for all mankind, as God spoke about His creation in Genesis 1. The devil especially wants to withhold hearts from knowing their true spiritual identity in Jesus Christ the Lord. Satan is the serpent of deception, destruction, and confusion.

Friend, this is why we need strong and mighty men and women of valor in these end times who will not break rank with God's holy plan in delivering the gospel of Jesus Christ to the world.

Many nations of the earth are becoming more demonized, demoralized, and desensitized as we are seeing the old cold serpent nature of Lucifer blind more hearts and minds with his cold and vile nature.

Being serious in ministry is the master's glory call upon your heart, and as you live in all the seriousness of heaven's chosen acceptance of God's holy ordination upon your life, the holy flames of fire will spread deeper in your obedient heart to become more like your true shepherd and His revealing truths as every heartbeat unfolds in your sold-out vessel.

Friend, choosing the fullness of Jesus Christ is the glorious life of total completion in Him. It is in the bridegroom chamber of the Father's heart where the glory of completion is spurring us on mightily in the Trinity union that burns our ministry destiny identity with great (Word of God) authority over all the works of darkness.

Psalm 119 30 (KJV), "I have chosen the way of truth: thy judgments have I laid before me."

Psalm 119:38 (KJV), "Stablish thy word unto thy servant, who is devoted to thy fear."

Some people are trying to redefine the gospel when they need to identify in the fullness of Jesus Christ of Nazareth and the fullness of the Holy Ghost, teaching it in all holiness with deep conviction and passion in the Holy Ghost's fire power.

We all must daily choose the footstool of Jesus Christ at the right hand of God, lie on the altar of His heart, and cry out for all souls, praying and interceding and fasting for them to be saved, for it is the ministry mandate for all who have answered the sacred call of the divine ordination of God Himself.

Friend, only truth will do, and its liberating power is for all to see and believe in free will. Make your choice today to be a sold-out servant of God in every defining way, as the ministry work is before you and the beckoning call of heaven to be ruthless against the powers of hell.

We are defined by the salvation of Christ. Therefore, let us labor in the attributes of our risen Savior and run with Jesus Christ's destiny identity, illuminating our hearts with the solid rock truth of the gospel message and the power of it, knowing that Jesus Christ alone is our eternal seal of redemption. God has no mistaken identity, as He has perfectly created the identity of all humanity and all living creatures. We need to daily choose what God says about our identity in His Holy Word instead of allowing the old serpent to poison hearts with deception and tormenting confusion, which always brings forth mass destruction of every kind of evil to the heart. Confusion is of the devil, not of God.

Heaven's Living Scroll, Jesus Christ

"The message of the cross is foolish to those who are headed for destruction! But we who are being saved know it is the very power of God" (1 Corinthians 1:18, NLT).

Jesus Christ is God's holy and living scroll that burns the heart with pure truth and raises up His chosen men and women to minister truth to all without doubt, fear, and unbelief.

Out of heaven, His scroll does flow down into the anointed hearts on the earth, writing and speaking the revelations of truth to bind up the broken-hearted and setting captives free.

A serious gospel is revealed for all to see, and the seriousness for chosen ministries is required to live in the throne room of all created life, where the heartbeat of God can minister powerful truths and warfare word strategies to His elect; they are the ministers of life and light and full proof of the supernatural nature of God manifesting in the earth.

> And there was delivered unto him the book of the prophet Esaias. And when he had opened the book, he found the place where it was written, The Spirit of the Lord is upon me, because he hath anointed me to preach the gospel to the poor; he hath sent me to heal the brokenhearted, to preach deliverance to the captives, and recovering of sight to the blind, to set at liberty them that are bruised, To preach the acceptable year of the Lord. And he closed the book, and he gave it again to the minister, and sat down. And the eyes of all them that were in the synagogue were fastened on him. And he began to say unto them, This day is this scripture fulfilled in your ears.
>
> Luke 4:17–21 (KJV)

May the serious ambassadors of Christ carry the flaming glory torch of heaven's liberty life force to all hearts with forerunner reality, speaking John the Baptist's words of impact, that the kingdom of heaven is at hand. Repentance is desperately needed, and the reverential fear of God returned to the church and to all the hearts of mankind.

In those days came John the Baptist, preaching in the wilderness of Judaea, And saying, Repent ye: for the kingdom of heaven is at hand. For this is he that was spoken of by the prophet Esaias, saying, The voice of one crying in the wilderness, Prepare ye the way of the Lord, make his paths straight. And the same John had his raiment of camel's hair, and a leathern girdle about his loins; and his meat was locusts and wild honey. Then went out to him Jerusalem, and all Judaea, and all the region round about Jordan, And were baptized of him in Jordan, confessing their sins. But when he saw many of the Pharisees and Sadducees come to his baptism, he said unto them, O generation of vipers, who hath warned you to flee from the wrath to come? Bring forth therefore fruits meet for repentance: And think not to say within yourselves, We have Abraham to our father: for I say unto you, that God is able of these stones to raise up children unto Abraham. And now also the axe is laid unto the root of the trees: therefore every tree which bringeth not forth good fruit is hewn down, and cast into the fire. I indeed baptize you with water unto repentance. but he that cometh after me is mightier than I, whose shoes I am not worthy to bear: he shall baptize you with the Holy Ghost, and with fire: Whose fan is in his hand, and he will throughly purge his floor, and gather his wheat into the garner; but he will burn up the chaff with unquenchable fire. Then cometh Jesus from Galilee to Jordan unto John, to be baptized of him. But John forbad him, saying, I have need to be baptized of thee, and comest thou to me? And Jesus answering said unto him, Suffer it to be so now: for thus it becometh us to fulfil all righteousness. Then he suffered him. And Jesus, when he was baptized, went up straightway out of the water: and, lo, the heavens were opened unto him, and he saw the Spirit of God descending like a dove, and lighting upon him: And lo a voice from heaven, saying, This is my beloved Son, in whom I am well pleased.

Matthew 3:1–17 (KJV)

Master of Ministry

The master wants to master your heart so He can master your life and ministry.

The apostles in the Holy Bible had all reverence for the living God and their holy shepherd, as they solely allowed Him to shepherd their hearts and master their lives and ministries. They strived to stay committed to the Word of God and the gospel message of Jesus as He brought correction to them as they needed it, just as He does with us in our day. However, Judas betrayed Jesus with a kiss, and self-destruction came upon his life. The apostles preached the resurrection power of Jesus Christ and His mandate of infallible truths with demonstrations of power but with much contention. God entrusted them with the gospel, as they were and are as an oracle of God before people.

Jesus Christ, the master of ministry, is the holy oracle of heaven that pierces the heart and all darkness with the supreme authority and power of His Holy Father. We can be raised up into the places of honor, speaking His Word with the Holy Ghost's boldness through His shining glory, thus demonstrating the power as well. As ministers of the gospel, we must allow the Lord to govern the ministry completely as we are all an open epistle before the word to see and read. Amen.

God wants sold-out Ministries that are unspotted from the world and purely teach His Word.

> Ye are our epistle written in our hearts, known and read of all men: Forasmuch as ye are manifestly declared to be the epistle of Christ ministered by us, written not

> with ink, but with the Spirit of the living God; not in tables of stone, but in fleshy tables of the heart.
>
> 2 Corinthians 3:2–3 (KJV)

These are powerful words from Apostle Paul, recorded for all of us to embrace and apply to our ministering hearts.

> For yourselves, brethren, know our entrance in unto you, that it was not in vain: But even after that we had suffered before, and were shamefully entreated, as ye know, at Philippi, we were bold in our God to speak unto you the gospel of God with much contention. For our exhortation was not of deceit, nor of uncleanness, nor in guile: But as we were allowed of God to be put in trust with the gospel, even so we speak; not as pleasing men, but God, which trieth our hearts. For neither at any time used we flattering words, as ye know, nor a cloke of covetousness; God is witness: Nor of men sought we glory, neither of you, nor yet of others, when we might have been burdensome, as the apostles of Christ. But we were gentle among you, even as a nurse cherisheth her children: So being affectionately desirous of you, we were willing to have imparted unto you, not the gospel of God only, but also our own souls, because ye were dear unto us. For ye remember, brethren, our labour and travail: for labouring night and day, because we would not be chargeable unto any of you, we preached unto you the gospel of God. Ye are witnesses, and God also, how holily and justly and unblameably we behaved ourselves among you that believe: As ye know how we exhorted and comforted and charged every one of you, as a father doth his children, That ye would walk worthy of God, who hath called you unto his kingdom and glory. For

this cause also thank we God without ceasing, because, when ye received the word of God which ye heard of us, ye received it not as the word of men, but as it is in truth, the word of God, which effectually worketh also in you that believe.

2 Thessalonians 2:1–13 (KJV)

Friend, I know I am using a lot of scriptures in this book, but I was taught by the Holy Ghost to magnify the Word of God before all peoples. I love magnifying His Word above all. When we do that, the anointing brings an increase. Christ, the anointed one, is the walking, living, breathing Word of the living God that engulfs the heart with the light of truth and must be first place above all things. The very heartbeats within our chest are for the Word of God to be magnified and glorified so we can forever abide in the holy presence of established praise and worship.

God upholds everything by the word of His power. See Hebrews 1:3.

Psalm 33:6 (KJV), "By the word of the Lord were the heavens made; and all the host of them by the breath of his mouth."

Master

Oh, in the wake of dawn and at nightfall, I always see Your glory light,

For I dwell under Your shadow and in Your saving delight.

I was told to go to the world and preach the gospel with power and purpose.

I humbly bow before You now and take the stand of upright authority in You before man.

The chosen ones are rising in the majestic plan of heaven's remnant force to destroy the works of the devil without carnal compromising.

The working of Your power empowers us to march forward with You as our rear guard and holy reward.

The only ministry that is truly successful is the crucified life in Christ flowing through our consecrated hearts unto our heavenly Father.

The finished works of Christ are covenant and completion.

Our master deserves all the glory, honor, and praise.

Oh, master of glory, holy and true, take us and use us for Your glory as we teach souls Your powerful love and enduring gospel of holiness.

The True Shepherd

The shepherd of the heart is a true shepherd, and we must teach this truth to all souls. The Lord spoke this to me many years ago about the true shepherd in Ezekiel 34.

> And the word of the Lord came unto me, saying, Son of man, prophesy against the shepherds of Israel, prophesy, and say unto them, Thus saith the Lord God unto the shepherds; Woe be to the shepherds of Israel that do feed themselves! should not the shepherds feed the flocks? Ye eat the fat, and ye clothe you with the wool, ye kill them that are fed: but ye feed not the flock.
>
> Ezekiel 34:1–3 (KJV)

The Lord spoke to me many years ago that He had had it with the pollution in the pulpits. Many are polluting the gospel for their own selfish gains, which will end up in a prideful fall and open shame. They are making it a compromising business instead of being about the heavenly Father's holy business.

The true shepherd wants the hearts of all who are in ministry to feed the sheep a feast from His royal throne of rich kingdom delicacies that cannot be manufactured by carnality.

Souls are hanging in the balance and are found wanting, and many are lost and dying as I'm typing this chapter. God forbid that His shepherds over flocks refuse the pure truth and turn hearts away from the sacred gospel because of bowing to seducing spirits and doctrines devils. See Daniel 5:27.

When one fails to preach the gospel as God directs, there will be a lack of knowledge and lack of power due to the unbelieving heart and the stiff neck of rebellious pride. See Hosea 4:6.

> And I will set up one shepherd over them, and he shall feed them, even my servant David; he shall feed them, and he shall be their shepherd. And I the Lord will be their God, and my servant David a prince among them; I the Lord have spoken it.
>
> Ezekiel 34:23–24 (KJV)

I encourage every minister and every chosen ministry to heed the divine order of God and set your face like a flint to seek out righteousness and justice. Righteous judgment is telling the pure truth of the living Word of God. What lines up with the Word of God is the righteousness of God.

Psalm 89:14 (KJV), "Justice and judgment are the habitation of thy throne: mercy and truth shall go before thy face."

True love is always telling the pure truth of God's Holy Word.

God never chose a coward to stand in the face of hell or in the face of the spirit of religion. He chose men and women who would *boldly speak the whole truth* without wavering and double-mindedness. We cannot truly represent heaven powerfully if we compromise with hell incorrectly and bow to the foreign gods of idolatry. What is not of God's holy kingdom and His Holy Word is as a foreign god to you.

Friend, how can we teach the gospel of Jesus Christ if we first don't live the gospel?

Teaching the Word, living the Word, and demonstrating it is our inherited sacred lot at the throne of God.

The Lord is saying this, "My child, come away with Me so I can shepherd your heart correctly so that you can shepherd My flock powerfully."

Friend, be about the heavenly Father's kingdom business, with Jesus leading the way in all truth with reverential fear. He is calling all ministries to the true shepherd's pattern of ministry.

The Lord spoke this word to me years ago, "Many were trying to patent the Holy Spirit instead of pattern their life after Him." We cannot tell God what we are going to preach; we must be an empty and humble vessel, allowing God to teach us holy truth and His plan for us individually, collectively, and corporately. His sheep and the lost souls need to hear the truth straight from heaven and His Holy Word.

Release the Sheep, Jesus Has Ownership

Friend, when we fully surrender to God in ministry, that does not make us a savior of lives. Jesus alone is the Savior and perfect intercessor, for He alone has *full ownership* of His sheep.

John 10:2 (KJV), "But he that entereth in by the door is the shepherd of the sheep."

When you have done your best, and you've laid down your life for your friend, and they still want God another way other than the holy teachings of the Bible, lay them at the feet of Jesus Christ and release them to Him. He will go after the one.

You pray, intercede, fast, and teach with great conviction, but you can never make someone love or serve God. Use wisdom. God knows hearts better than any human ever will.

Jesus Christ owns His sheep; therefore, as ministers, we must never desire to control and be possessive and manipulate souls, for that type of behavior is not the nature of Jesus Christ.

If a sheep goes astray, this is what the true shepherd will do,

> For the Son of man is come to save that which was lost. How think ye? if a man have an hundred sheep, and one of them be gone astray, doth he not leave the ninety and nine, and goeth into the mountains, and seeketh that which is gone astray? And if so be that he find it, verily I say unto you, he rejoiceth more of that sheep, than of the ninety and nine which went not astray. Even so it is not the will of your Father which is in heaven, that one of these little ones should perish.
>
> Matthew 18:11–14 (KJV)

Friend, be the flaming torch of heaven so that people on the earth will be stirred in heart to desire God to the fullest and become swift to repent, wanting Jesus Christ as their Lord and Savior.

Holy, holy, holy, holy is the Lord Almighty!

Strong Leadership

A strong leader leads well and subdues all opposing forces of hell before them.

Friend, strong leaders are led by the Holy Spirit. They are keen on spiritual vision. They lack nothing and possess all things in the spiritual goodness of God. They are hated for speaking and standing by the written Word of God.

The qualities of strong leaders attending to the teachings of God's Word will never compromise nor coward down to the devil and the spirit of religion. A strong leader stands and feeds on the strength of the Almighty God when standing before a cold and demoralized world that is filled with the contentious carnal dust of fallen man.

"As sorrowful, yet always rejoicing; as poor, yet making many rich; as having nothing, and yet possessing all things" (2 Corinthians 6:10, KJV).

Strong leaders are always ostracized for living in and teaching the characteristics of Jesus Christ's nature. They defy the powers of hell and the spirit of religion, for they know the high price for the anointing, and they willingly pay it with their dear lives if need be.

God is looking for strong leaders who will lead people in the wealth of spiritual holiness and the strong conviction of the holy truth of Jesus Christ's saving power, whereby all men must be saved!

Strong leaders live life investing in lives, as they see the need for the presence of God to be richly dwelling in the hearts of mankind. Strong leaders take a stronghold of the Word of God and have a continuous feast of the hidden manna from the heart of God to share with hungry and thirsty souls. Strong leaders never lay down their swords in battle because the sword is their strong defense and victory over all opposing forces against Jesus Christ—the infallible living Word. Strong leaders are the fearless few who see afar and warn with the warnings of heaven. Strong leaders have rich discernment, which is a guiding principle that keeps the heart in check and well-balanced as they daily adhere to the biblical truths of God's infallible Word.

Man-made Ministries—Wolves Mentality

A man-made ministry is not a God-ordained ministry. Remember, what is man-made becomes marred; what is God-made becomes a beautiful vessel of honor.

Friend, man-made ministries grieve the Holy Spirit and corrupt lives with the confused and deceptive nature of Satan. A man-made ministry never feeds the sheep; they ravish them of the spiritual nourishment of pure truth, teaching a seductive demonized doctrine that leads many astray without feeling remorse.

> Take heed therefore unto yourselves, and to all the flock, over the which the Holy Ghost hath made you overseers, to feed the church of God, which he hath purchased with his own blood. For I know this, that after my departing shall grievous wolves enter in among you, not sparing the flock. Also of your own selves shall men arise, speaking perverse things, to draw away disciples after them.
>
> Acts 20:28–30 (KJV)

What is not God-made will become a pile of defeated ashes consumed by the holy fire of truth.

Matthew 15:14 (KJV), "Let them alone: they be blind leaders of the blind. And if the blind lead the blind, both shall fall into the ditch."

Don't follow a spiritually blind leader because there will always be a death cycle of spiritual death and depravity.

Friend, don't be defiled by the ways of the world and the cunning craftiness of man or woman. Do not allow unbelief and the traditions of man to pull your heart away from God and be bewitched into believing a lie that can seduce your soul into hell.

> That we henceforth be no more children, tossed to and fro, and carried about with every wind of doctrine, by the sleight of men, and cunning craftiness, whereby they lie in wait to deceive; But speaking the truth in love, may grow up into him in all things, which is the head, even Christ: From whom the whole body fitly joined together and compacted by that which every joint supplieth, according to the effectual working in the measure of every part, maketh increase of the body unto the edifying of itself in love.
>
> Ephesians 4:14–16 (KJV)

God never created cults and confusion; He created an everlasting covenant of infallible truth. God is a covenant of truth that is everlasting and powerful in its kingdom right.

Genesis 17:7 (KJV), "And I will establish my covenant between me and thee and thy seed after thee in their generations for an everlasting covenant, to be a God unto thee, and to thy seed after thee."

To all ministers and ministries, I am imploring to you through the sure mercies of God that you lie before God's holy face at the throne of grace, asking Him to search your heart and reveal to you if you are teaching and preaching and speaking as an oracle of God, representing His kingdom in all truth and all sincerity, in holiness and trembling at His Word.

On Prophesying

If you have the gift of prophecy, it must always be *truth*, only Truth. Don't pollute the gospel by speaking lies.

The Lord spoke this to me many years ago, "Much of the prophecies today are pathetic before My throne." If you are seeking a word from the Lord, open your Bible, listen to the Holy Spirit, and trust Him to speak to you.

God does use His prophets to prophesy as I, too, have the gift of prophecy. However, there is a grave deception that has invaded many churches, as some are seeking a word from a man or woman every service over hearing from the true prophet, Jesus Christ. May I say we must always seek the giver of gifts and not place any spiritual gifts above the written Word of God. Never place any of God's sacred gifts above His greatest gift, Jesus Christ (*the holy* and *living Word of God*.) Jesus is the gift that keeps on giving so we can go on living.

The Lord gave me this word on February 6, 2018: Some people are so busy looking for a word from man that they are losing focus of the written Word of God left to mankind.

Prophecy is a beautiful gift that must be orchestrated by the Spirit of God. I am thankful for the wonderful true prophets that are in the world today who are an oracle of God.

Devils come as angels of light.

> Then the Lord said unto me, The prophets prophesy lies in my name: I sent them not, neither have I commanded them, neither spake unto them: they prophesy unto you a false vision and divination, and a thing of nought, and the deceit of their heart.
>
> Jeremiah 14:14 (KJV)

> For such are false apostles, deceitful workers, transforming themselves into the apostles of Christ. And no marvel; for Satan himself is transformed into an angel of light. Therefore it is no great thing if his ministers also be transformed as the ministers of righteousness; whose end shall be according to their works.
>
> 2 Corinthians 11:13–15 (KJV)

May the end of our works be justified by grace and in full righteousness and holiness as we may hear the Lord say on that faithful and noble day, "Well done, thou good and faithful servant."

True ministries tremble at God's Word and read it in strong conviction, applying all words to their surrendered heart in the perfect will of God, their creator.

Jesus Christ is the true prophet who will always tell you all the full proof of truth.

God has given many gifts to His children, which is glorious. We must operate in the gifts, as the validations of Christ demonstrate through our vessels. Amen.

CHAPTER 15: EXPOSING IDOLS

A Word Famine in the Heart and Land

There is a serious word famine in the land because there are too many idols present in the hearts of mankind.

> And we know that we are of God, and the whole world lieth in wickedness. And we know that the Son of God is come, and hath given us an understanding, that we may know him that is true, and we are in him that is true, even in his Son Jesus Christ. This is the true God, and eternal life. Little children, keep yourselves from idols. Amen.
>
> 1 John 5:19–21 (KJV)

When we keep ourselves from idols and stay true to the Word, it is constant freedom from the hard bondages of carnality.

Friend, we are in a day and time where many people want the world and its idolatrous ways over the Holy Word of God. Anything we put before God can become an idol in our hearts. The whole earth is filled with idols, and God wants to remove all idols from the hearts of mankind so He can flood them with the words of Spirit life and abundant life in Jesus Christ.

Idols are a constant death cycle that steals from the heart the spirit life of living in the joys of Jesus Christ's abundant life force. When people crave idols over truth, the enemy forces a greater demand for the selfish position of false fulfillment, hence holding the heart captive with a diabolic invasion that resists the knowledge of God's proven truths. We must keep ourselves from all lying idols and daily perform a heart search before the throne of grace because we must become the reflection of truth and the attributes of Jesus Christ.

Our heavenly Father wants our pure hearts on display on the world's stage, showing all peoples, great and small, the reality of Jesus Christ living to the fullest in our free vessels carrying His glory, with godliness to those souls that are desperate and hungry for truth and not carnal idols that carry the heart away into all the lust of the flesh. The pollutants of idols always cause stagnation to the spirit with its carnal corruption of hard bondage to the heart.

We look for the Word across land and sea, searching for the truth of heaven that shines ever so present in the hearts of the children of the cross of Christ. The invaluable words of life capture the heart and rapture it into the throne room of divine love, where idols have no accepted existence. Still, the abundant realities of Jesus Christ's spiritual nourishment produce all the wealth and riches tried and true in the golden glory realm of our heavenly Father's treasured Word.

> Not unto us, O Lord, not unto us, but unto thy name give glory, for thy mercy, and for thy truth's sake. Wherefore should the heathen say, Where is now their God? But our God is in the heavens: he hath done whatsoever he hath pleased. Their idols are silver and gold, the work of men's hands. They have mouths, but they speak not: eyes have they, but they see not: They have ears, but they hear not: noses have they, but they smell not: They have hands, but they handle not: feet have they, but they walk not: neither speak they through their throat. They that make them are like unto them; so is every one that trusteth in them.
>
> Psalm 115:1–8 (KJV)

> Cursed be the man that maketh any graven or molten image, an abomination unto the Lord, the work of the hands of the craftsman, and putteth it in a secret place. And all the people shall answer and say, Amen.
>
> Deuteronomy 27:15 (KJV)

Friend, years ago, God spoke a word to me about the end times. He said there is a Word famine in the land, as there was a famine in the days of Joseph. Egypt was a land full of idols and lacked the desire to follow hard after God and His righteous ways. Pride and arrogance ruled many hearts and contaminated the spirit of mankind, therefore leaving the soul in the bewildered state of the demonic control of hell's poisonous lies of carnal works and committing abominations against the one true living God.

Idols are empty and worthless things that steal from the heart of mankind the glorious beauty of knowing richly the king of glory and His holy treasures that are invaluable.

Friend, we must never allow any form of an idol to overpower our flesh and invade our hearts, as they will ultimately destroy and deprive the heart of wholesome living uprightly before God. Idols are an abomination and a stench in God's nostrils. God hates idols and the pride that accompanies them, but He loves a humble heart in search of His living truth and saving power.

His Quickening Spirit Is Your Awakening Life

God wants to quicken your mortal body into the supernatural life of His holy resurrection power, raising you up in the liberation of the guiding force of the supernatural nature of His Son Jesus Christ. Hence, the perfection of His radiant image shines His rewarding glory within your idol-free vessel in the throne room of heaven. God quickens us to awaken us to greater depths and heights in His kingdom life of the supernatural education that quickens us with the awakenings of wealth upon wealth, as we can never stay where we are in our spiritual journey because there is always constant change, constant growth, and fresh manna to break with the master at the throne of grace. God gives us a little here and a little there that manifest in the greater abundance of spirit life. We can't absorb the Word of God in one single day, but we can partake of His royal feast in the allotted process of growth as designed in our Father's perfect will.

I had a powerful encounter with the Lord in South Bend, Indiana, while in a church service. I was graciously worshipping the Lord, and I had my hands raised up high to Him, and my mind was solely upon my glorious Savior. Then, suddenly, the presence of God came rushing powerfully within my body with such powerful glory fire and His authoritative Word, moving with a swift force and such surging of His anointing, quickening, also with such an explosive force of power that I literally had to ask God to lift His tangible, all-mighty presence from within my spirit and body, for, you see, I literally felt in my *physical body* that I could *die* as my body could not handle this mighty visitation of His forever reigning glory.

God wanted to show me that just a small supernatural touch of His magnificent and *dunamis* power can literally kill the physical body. You see, I felt like every cell in my body would explode into smithereens to the point that I begged and begged Him to lift this powerful touch from my physical body. I also felt as if His glory was surging within my vessel of how He was allowing this to happen to me for a greater purpose. I now understand one purpose is to share with all of you so you will always be hungry and thirsty for the greatness of His all-mighty power because no worthless idol can bring a heart into the intimate fiery fellowship with the creator of heaven and Earth. I will say to you that this holy experience was truly one of the greatest supernatural encounters in my life thus far. It was truly unspeakable and full of intimate glory wonders. Our spirits can obtain an allotted portion by portion. God is extremely powerful beyond imagination.

God awakened my spirit to the greater revelations of reverential fear and greater glory realms of the increasing anointing that was supernaturally given to me.

Some may read this and say, "I don't believe that."

Friend, may I say to you, "You will if it happens to you."

Isn't that so true? Unbelief is like an idol to many hearts because it is directed by pride and the blinding control of the flesh. I truly pray that you have glorious encounters with the heavenly Father, as He loves to reveal Himself to people.

Friend, another purpose for this encounter was to let me know where my heart stood with my master, as I always flow in the child-like faith to simply believe Him for every supernatural fiery wonder that He has set apart for my life as I have craved His supernatural nature my entire life.

The lovely and wonderful nature of God is most glorious. My heart condition before His throne is this: no idols of contamination, no characteristics of pride, no withholding of my vessel from His perfect works of daily transforming the heart into the divine nature of our glorious master, Jesus Christ our Lord.

God looks upon the heart, and when we depart for this old world, all that we are taking with us is what we have within our hearts.

Psalm 44:21(KJV), "Shall not God search this out? for he knoweth the secrets of the heart."

> But if the Spirit of him that raised up Jesus from the dead dwell in you, he that raised up Christ from the dead shall also quicken your mortal bodies by his Spirit that dwelleth in you. Therefore, brethren, we are debtors, not to the flesh, to live after the flesh.
>
> Romans 8:11–12 (KJV)

John 6:63 (KJV), "It is the spirit that quickeneth; the flesh profiteth nothing: the words that I speak unto you, they are spirit, and they are life."

Friend, as we stay spirit to Spirit before God and heed His quickening ways, the flesh is subdued under our feet in every way. You can live in the presence of God, free from idols, as you keep your heart in the ways of truth and in complete surrender to God.

The most important thing that you have in your heart and hand is the written Word of God. Heed the heavenly Father's quickening of truth.

Living idolatry-free is staying in the life-giving Word, keeping it first place in the heart.

Psalm 73:26 (KJV), "My flesh and my heart faileth: but God is the strength of my heart, and my portion for ever."

Pride Is an Idol within Itself

The Lord spoke these words to me many years ago, "Pride, the big I, the big lie."

Pride doesn't want I AM that I AM to be in charge, oh no. Pride wants control of everything and over all things because the big I has partnered up with hell and the deceitful words of Lucifer. See Isaiah 14.

Lucifer was so busy telling God about what the big I of spiritual pride was going to do that the thrusting out of God's power destroyed Lucifer's heavenly ranking and cast him out of heaven.

Refuse natural pride and spiritual pride and live a harmonious life with the Trinity.

Friend, the more people say, "I will do as I please," the more one misses the will of God and His glorious benefits of rewarding humble obedience before His throne.

The devil knows the weaknesses of all humanity and how to tempt the heart into disobeying God and His Word. The devil is filled with the lie of the big I. Pride is one of the biggest snares the devil brings to trap a heart into rebellious sin and its blinding wickedness. Pride constricts and imprisons the heart with the heavy chains of hell's deceitful enslavements, so it fully operates in the evil workings of exerting control over others yet having no self-control over their own life or spirit.

Pride is a liar that denies the heart of the kingdom authenticity, therefore robbing the heart of true and lasting fulfillment while living on the earth. We always need to seek to be God's close friend and not that of an appalling enemy nature, but for the just cause of having a holy habitation with Him for all eternity. He is the mighty judge in all supreme authority that has the power to banish a soul from His presence into outer darkness. We sure don't want that to happen to any *soul*. Amen. The sad truth is some will never let their pride go and yield their hearts to the mercy and grace of God in order to be saved by the love and power of Jesus Christ.

Have mercy, Lord. Have mercy, for we don't want *one* soul to perish.

Pride is filled with the world's ways of craving accolades, titles, and status. Humility throws all earthly and spiritual achievements at the feet of Jesus and is promoted into the greater realms of glory fire life. Pride will drag a heart down the path of the wickedness. Humility will keep the heart following Jesus Christ and trembling at His Word.

Proverbs 4:14 (KJV), "Enter not into the path of the wicked, and go not in the way of evil men."

Proverbs 4:18–19 (KJV), "But the path of the just is as the shining light, that shineth more and more unto the perfect day. The way of the wicked is as darkness: they know not at what they stumble."

Humility will always bring heaven's perfection to the heart, as heaven is perfect in love, while pride is disgraceful and ruthlessly defined by the cold serpent nature of Satan.

Pride is a carnal reality that carves a Pharaoh mentality. Pride is a dark plague to the heart because it is likened to the hard heart of Pharaoh in the book of Exodus. God gave Pharaoh the ten plagues because of his wickedness of pride and idolatry and gave Moses the ten commandments for a holy way of living for the Hebrew children.

> For the invisible things of him from the creation of the world are clearly seen, being understood by the things that are made, even his eternal power and Godhead; so that they are without excuse: Because that, when they knew God, they glorified him not as God, neither were thankful; but became vain in their imaginations, and their foolish heart was darkened. Professing themselves to be wise, they became fools, And changed the glory of the uncorruptible God into an image made like to corruptible man, and to birds, and fourfooted beasts, and creeping things. Wherefore God also gave them up to uncleanness through the lusts of their own hearts, to dishonour their own bodies between themselves: Who changed the truth of God into a lie, and worshipped and served the creature more than the Creator, who is blessed for ever. Amen.
>
> Romans 1:20–25 (KJV)

Friend, this is what pride does; it is an idol within itself, and it's perplexing in nature to see this invasion of hell take over a man or woman and watch them fall prey to the ravishing demonic infiltration that poisons the heart, choking out all spiritual life.

Pride Hates Instructions

> And say, How have I hated instruction, and my heart despised reproof; And have not obeyed the voice of my teachers, nor inclined mine ear to them that instructed me! I was almost in all evil in the midst of the congregation and assembly.
>
> Proverbs 5:12–14 (KJV)

Friend, there is such an evil invasion against truth in the church and in the whole earth. Demonic invasions have increased, and souls are falling into the lies of pride as they refuse to listen to truth as they are demanding their own ways of rebellion and sin.

The evil is right in our faces, spewing out cruelty against the ones that deliver truth.

I am personally witnessing the increase of people refusing to obey God and heed His warnings because the invasions of pride have distorted their thinking into placing their heart on pride's know-it-all platform, where they have the audience of one, which is the empty idol of I. Many are abandoning God's instructions to establish their own self-destructive instructions.

God Hates a Proud Look

Friend, we should hate what God hates and not tolerate the works of evil but reprove them. Love the soul but hate the sin. Amen!

Pride is an abomination before God; it toxifies the heart and cripples the mind and spirit with spiritual malnutrition. Pride will always shed innocent blood because pride is always self-serving, not God-serving. Pride always leads to mischief because one never grows up in the spirit as they prefer being the king or queen of their own sandbox castle while they live in defiance of the kingdom of God.

> These six things doth the Lord hate: yea, seven are an abomination unto him: A proud look, a lying tongue, and hands that shed innocent blood, An heart that deviseth wicked imaginations, feet that be swift in running to mischief, A false witness that speaketh lies, and he that soweth discord among brethren.
>
> Proverbs 6:16–19 (KJV)

Pride Has No Need for God

Pride says, "I have no need for God, for I will be as my own god. I will do as I please, as I only answer to self."

Pride has no reverential fear of God; in fact, it refuses to revere God and His supreme authority. Pride is a ruthless lie that produces the way of darkness and its invasions of lying vanities.

Jonah 2:8 (KJV), "They that observe lying vanities forsake their own mercy."

Pride can't run and hide from God, for He knows where every living heart beats on the earth. Those who say they have no need for God and His righteous ways may they rethink that heart action and ponder God's lovingkindness and tender mercies that have allowed life in their bodies and flooded hope within their hearts so they could humbly bow in repentance and turn from the idol of selfish pride, never to return to the sin nature of it but instead choose to live a life in humility and drink from the rivers of God's holy delight. Amen! Friend, there is much to be done for the kingdom's sake and souls to be won, as God wants to use saved hearts mightily for His glory in selfless surrender.

Pride shows no mercy; it produces misery upon misery in the heart and living in a spiritual death cycle twenty-four seven, 365 days a year.

Pride produces an evil heart of unbelief and is carried away like the chaff blowing in the wind.

Pride reaps unwanted spiritual afflictions of self-inflicted pain. God wants to set free the heart that is filled with pride.

Pride wears a mask of self-deception and the vile works of iniquity that cannot be hidden no matter the covering of the mask. Pride masquerades a false identity that parades hell's agenda of evil arrogance and a stiff-necked mentality.

Pride is one of the greatest tools of Satan, as it is prevalent in the lands. Pride is of a hostile nature against God. Pride demands its own lying right, which is always selfishly wrong. Pride lives a life of dishonesty and discontent.

Friend, when we strive to live as God has designed for us to live, we will not choose a life of dishonesty and fraudulent behaviors that lead to foolishness and worthlessness.

Our heavenly Father has given us thousands of thousands of sacred scriptures to live by, and we can live by them as we apply them daily to our sold-out hearts. We take our humble vessels before the throne of grace in all honesty and selflessness, believing that more wisdom and knowledge will richly flow in our hearts and develop a beautiful and productive lifestyle that is well-pleasing before our heavenly Father.

> The Lord detests the use of dishonest scales, but he delights in accurate weights. Pride leads to disgrace, but with humility comes wisdom. Honesty guides good people; dishonesty destroys treacherous people. Riches won't help on the day of judgment, but right living can save you from death. The godly are directed by honesty; the wicked fall beneath their load of sin. The godliness

of good people rescues them; the ambition of treacherous people traps them. When the wicked die, their hopes die with them, for they rely on their own feeble strength. The godly are rescued from trouble, and it falls on the wicked instead.

Proverbs 11:1–8 (NLT)

Pride is a foolish condition of the heart before the throne of grace. Pride hates accountability and wants to hold onto the old nature of fallen man.

Make sure you get right before God now by repenting and putting everything under the blood of the Lamb because when we stand before God on judgment day, it will be way too late then to try to make things right. Amen. In this chapter, I have covered idols and pride for a reason. Idols and pride are rampant on the earth, not only with the lost but also with some brothers and sisters in Christ.

It's Time to Move Forward

Friend, a spiritual heart examination and true repentance are a wonderful practice and should be addressed daily before the throne of grace by humbling yourself before God and asking Him to expose everything that needs to be exposed within your heart so you can be 100 percent sure that you are in the holy place of living in His perfect will and not grieving His Holy Spirit by anything that is not of His righteous ways. Our hearts need to have a clean sweep every day. A clean heart leads to a holy lifestyle.

God specializes in examining one's life and heart because there is always a righteous lifeline of truth through the redemption and deliverance of His Son, Jesus, who took away the sins of the world. He is here to take away all sins in every repentant heart. When a soul is set free from the invasion of pride, the Lord wants to use that heart for great and mighty things, as all have sinned and fallen short of the glory of God.

Romans 3:23 (KJV), "For all have sinned, and come short of the glory of God."

Repentance is a beautiful thing; it transforms the heart in the holy wonders of our forgiving king of glory. How refreshing to know that God always provides a fresh start for all repentant and sincere hearts that want truth and righteousness over the ways of the world and the pride of life. You can be all that God alone has called and chosen you to be. Hell cannot have you, destroy you, or steal from you anymore. In Jesus' name! Amen! Oh, what intimate glory from above that sets a heart in a joyous and liberating place of rich fulfillment in the attributes of Jesus Christ.

Friend, it's time to wisely and powerfully thrive in the great things of God. Step up, step out, and burn powerfully for the master. Souls are awaiting your anointed arrival in the harvest field. Son and daughter of God, the Lord wants you to be the genuine you that He created you to be. He wants to take you farther than you have been before and use you greatly for His glory. There are many souls out there that are lost and hurting and hungry and thirsty that need Jesus Christ's Spirit life that is alive in you!

Live in the Light

Live in the light, as he is the light, where pride and idols cannot dwell.

> For this ye know, that no whoremonger, nor unclean person, nor covetous man, who is an idolater, hath any inheritance in the kingdom of Christ and of God. Let no man deceive you with vain words: for because of these things cometh the wrath of God upon the children of disobedience. Be not ye therefore partakers with them. For ye were sometimes darkness, but now are ye

light in the Lord: walk as children of light: (For the fruit of the Spirit is in all goodness and righteousness and truth;) Proving what is acceptable unto the Lord. And have no fellowship with the unfruitful works of darkness, but rather reprove them. For it is a shame even to speak of those things which are done of them in secret. But all things that are reproved are made manifest by the light: for whatsoever doth make manifest is light. Wherefore he saith, Awake thou that sleepest, and arise from the dead, and Christ shall give thee light.

Ephesians 5:5–14 (KJV)

CHAPTER 16: MY CHILD, COME UP HITHER

His Supernatural Nature Is Calling You

God wants us to live in the Spirit of the Lord every day.

Revelation 1:10 (KJV), "I was in the Spirit on the Lord's day, and heard behind me a great voice, as of a trumpet."

Revelation 4:1 (KJV),

> After this I looked, and, behold, a door was opened in heaven: and the first voice which I heard was as it were of a trumpet talking with me; which said, Come up hither, and I will shew thee things which must be hereafter.

We are living in the very book of Revelation right now. It is a powerful book of the manifestations of the supernatural nature of Jesus Christ. God loves to reveal Himself to us in supernatural ways, and I pray when you read these powerful encounters that I have had with the Spirit of the Lord, that they will encourage you to come up higher in your faith and rich hunger for the deeper things in the Holy Spirit and the Holy Word. Embrace the supernatural and the higher education of the Holy Bible, for it is truly set apart just for you. Be a believer and a receiver, not a doubter and a pouter. Faith is living and always rewarded; doubt, on the other hand, is worthless and void of substance.

Friend, this last and final chapter addresses the end-time church of Jesus Christ, who is to be operating in the fullness of Him as we are not a church of man-made labels and religious fables. We are not to be separated by man-made doctrines or the blinding invasions of the spirit of religion that cause a heart to be held captive by false doctrines of heavy taskmaster's control and manipulations that are a killing force fueled by the works of hell and the doctrines of demons. We are to be one *bride* and one *body* of *Christ*, as we have only one Lord, one Savior, and one baptism. Amen.

Men and women created lukewarm churches and divisions; Jesus established the *church* and requires unity in the body of Christ.

The salvation of Jesus Christ to usward came through the shedding of His own blood, not anything else. He is the sacrificed lamb of God and He has set up the very spiritual foundation of righteousness and holiness for all Christians to live by and to also richly apply to their humble and obedient hearts.

Ephesians 4:4–6 (KJV), "There is one body, and one Spirit, even as ye are called in one hope of your calling; One Lord, one faith, one baptism, One God and Father of all, who is above all, and through all, and in you all."

We welcome You, Holy Spirit! We will not hinder You, quench You, stifle You, or resist You! We most certainly will not stand in Your way. We welcome You to have Your most holy way in our midst today. In Jesus' mighty name and the Holy Ghost's fame.

Caught up in the Spirit of the Lord

Zechariah 2:5 (KJV), "For I, saith the Lord, will be unto her a wall of fire round about, and will be the glory in the midst of her."

Friend, in the early 1980s, while in my bed sleeping, I was caught up in the Spirit of the Lord. I was completely in the spirit and moving in swift acceleration, going upward into the galaxies and the darkness of the sky. I was taken to a very huge platform suspended in the heavenlies, where suddenly my feet hit the top of the platform, and I was standing upright only to be taught by the Holy Spirit about the condition of much of His church today.

I saw to the right of me some adult-size naked babies that were lying on the platform, completely asleep. They were all obese, but I could not identify which were male or female because God, in His perfect wisdom, did not show that to me. I saw in front of me, just a few feet away, demons (disembodied creatures) that had their eyes watching the adult-size babies, making sure they stayed in the slumbering state, never to wake up. Their assignment from hell was to babysit the adult-sized babies because they did not want them to wake up. If they woke up out of their slumber to learn who and what they are in Jesus Christ, the principalities would be totally defeated and dismantled of their wicked plans against the children of God.

As I was observing all of this, they began to look at me. I was completely in the Holy Spirit's protection, authority, and power of God. There was no fear of the demons in my vessel, as we are not to fear any devil! Amen!

I knew these were high-ranking principalities that had much of the body of Christ asleep and very lazy. In my observation, while in the spirit seeing this powerful encounter, the Lord was speaking to my spirit that the babies represented much of the church in our day and how it is sleeping and terribly lazy.

The beauty in the powerful experience was that I was fully engulfed in the glory of God. The demonic forces could not touch me, and they knew that I had all authority over them through Jesus Christ's mighty power and in His magnificent and omnipotent name and kingdom fame.

The adult-size babies mean they all thought they were *grown* and *mature* in the Lord, but they were not. All they wanted was the salvation experience and not the crucified life of dying to the rotten flesh mess and its wicked desires of worldly lust of all kinds. They were carnal and lukewarm in nature and gravely deceived by the devil but thought they were so close to God. They were so charmed and deceived by the powers of hell that they didn't know they were naked and blind.

The obese adult babies were not clothed in the glory because they craved the things of the flesh and the ways of the world more than the Word and Spirit of God. The nakedness represents the carnal nature of man, the lust of the flesh, and the pride of life.

They were obese because they were only drinking the sincere milk of the Word and refusing to pay the price for the greater education in Word and spirit. They had doubt, fear, and unbelief in their hearts. They wanted a pacifier to soothe their flesh instead of having the sword of the Lord flowing from their lips. They were not maturing in the meat of the Word and in the Spirit of God because they were too lazy to seek out the hidden manna and wealthy treasures in the inner chamber of God's heart of all truth and holiness.

In their place, slumber and idleness brought a folding of the hands that kept them from being awakened and alerted to the end-time greater works of Jesus Christ, their glorious Messiah. They were being robbed of their ministry destiny identities and their missions and mandates from being fulfilled.

They did not know the hostile spiritual warfare works of hell that took them hostage.

In their slumbering state, they could not be fully awakened in spirit and truth so that they could collectively and corporately have a profound impact on souls. They were also being taught false doctrines that placed them in a slumbering place of carnal works that stifled their growth due to the lack of knowledge. They refused to work out their own salvation with fear and trembling. They coveted the anointing and gifts of others due to not knowing their own authentic identity in Jesus Christ's salvation lifestyle. They chose rebellion and disobedience over complete surrender and obedience.

He that hath an ear, let him hear what the Spirit saith unto the churches. And unto the angel of the church of the Laodiceans write; These things saith the Amen, the faithful and true witness, the beginning of the creation of God; I know thy works, that thou art neither cold nor hot: I would thou wert cold or hot. So then because thou art lukewarm, and neither cold nor hot, I will spue thee out of my mouth. Because thou sayest, I am rich, and increased with goods, and have need of nothing; and knowest not that thou art wretched, and miserable, and poor, and blind, and naked: I counsel thee to buy of me gold tried in the fire, that thou mayest be rich; and white raiment, that thou mayest be clothed, and that the shame of thy nakedness do not appear; and anoint thine eyes with eyesalve, that thou mayest see. As many as I love, I rebuke and chasten: be zealous therefore, and repent. Behold, I stand at the door, and knock: if any man hear my voice, and open the door, I will come in to him, and will sup with him, and he with me. To him that overcometh will I grant to sit with me in my throne, even as I also overcame, and am set down with my Father in his throne.

> Revelation 3:13–21 (KJV)

Wake up, glorious church! Wake up now before it's too late. The alarm is sounding; it's ringing out for a worldwide wake-up call. Get up, dry bones, and become a glorious and vast army! Note: Ezekiel 37:1–14.

Our king is coming. He is coming for a bride that is without spot or wrinkle! Oh, church, clothe yourselves with praise and prayer. The master is visiting hearts. He is calling on His people to become demonstrators of supernatural things. Open the chapters of His eternal love letter, and as you turn the chapters of His heart, believe its Word, do His will, speak out, and proclaim, for His day is drawing near. Take a step of faith by walking His holy highway in your destiny identity and reap the holy backing of heaven as you will be led in every step by the Holy Spirit's unction and revelations of Jesus Christ.

Dismantling Hell's Army

Amos 5:10 (KJV), "They hate him that rebuketh in the gate, and they abhor him that speaketh uprightly."

Friend, many years ago, in an open vision, the Lord revealed to me hell's army. It was massive, and every disembodied demon creature was vile in nature, as they were marching forcefully toward me with an extremely cold reptile nature of cruel hatred in their blackest of black eyes. I knew full well within my soul; it was evident that all this hate was hell's hatred for the Spirit of Jesus Christ and His kingdom that was alive and reigning within my vessel. I was engulfed in the glory of God without fear. God had me standing still in total observation of this powerful time of great supernatural education. Every single demon was completely powerless to the Spirit of Jesus Christ within my vessel.

I knew I was a threat to hell itself and that every demon wanted me dead and removed from the face of the earth because they knew that I was a child of God and that I was here walking out my destiny identity by taking the gospel to the nations. They could not stop me on any given scale. They wanted to destroy me completely in any way that they could. They could not touch me, as I was clothed in the very armor of God and the radiance of the glory from on high.

The Lord had me in such keen spiritual observation of their movement as they were completely in full synchronization with every movement of motion. They operated in complete unity and with one known agenda, which was to destroy me.

Lucifer and every fallen angel with him are attempting to ultimately destroy every human on Earth, especially those who are born-again Christians. Friend, the devil is real, and he is the great deceiver that has deceived many for centuries. He is a liar, and he is defeated!

When this vision happened to me, the Lord spoke to me that He was going to use me to raise up an army in this nation. A great harvest of souls will be harvested for the kingdom of God around the world. It is end-time revival time, as in the flaming glory of the early church in the book of Acts!

We are in very hostile spiritual warfare, and many are blinded to it, including many in the church, but the Christians must arise in the anointing power of Jesus Christ and exercise their authority over all the powers of darkness. Our battles are not to be against one another but against the powers of darkness that attack humanity. We should all be encouraging one another to live for God more than ever before!

God is raising up His sold-out army to dismantle hell's army in the power of love and in the power of His Holy Spirit. I thank God for His heavenly hosts that are for us! Amen. See 2 Kings chapter 6.

> Put on the whole armour of God, that ye may be able to stand against the wiles of the devil. For we wrestle not against flesh and blood, but against principalities, against powers, against the rulers of the darkness of this world, against spiritual wickedness in high places. Wherefore take unto you the whole armour of God, that ye may be able to withstand in the evil day, and having done all, to stand. Stand therefore, having your loins girt about with truth, and having on the breastplate of righteousness; And your feet shod with the preparation of the gospel of peace; Above all, taking the shield of faith, wherewith ye shall be able to quench all the fiery darts of the wicked. And take the helmet of salvation, and the

> sword of the Spirit, which is the word of God: Praying always with all prayer and supplication in the Spirit, and watching thereunto with all perseverance and supplication for all saints.
>
> Ephesians 6:11–18 (KJV)

Use your armor. Use it skillfully, as it is the serious truth that wins on all battle fronts. The armor of God is an armor of light, as Jesus is the light of the world!

It is glory fire light.

Glory—God's manifested presence, Jesus Christ, and the Holy Spirit.

Glory—John 1:14 (KJV), "And the Word was made flesh, and dwelt among us, (and we beheld his glory, the glory as of the only begotten of the Father,) full of grace and truth."

Fire—Hebrews 12:29 (KJV), "For our God is a consuming fire."

Light—John 8:12 (KJV), "Then spake Jesus again unto them, saying, I am the light of the world: he that followeth me shall not walk in darkness, but shall have the light of life."

Friend, all of hell cannot stop you. No flesh can stop you because God is with you and for you! Amen!

Mount Up, Army of the Lord!

We are dressed for battle twenty-four seven, 365 days a year. We wear the uncompromising holy fire revival attire from on high!

Mount up, army. We are riding strong every day, empowered by the Word of the Lord and His Holy Spirit.

The Army of the Lord

The Lord gave me this word years ago: We are the blood-bought, sold-out, set-apart, 100 percent victorious army of the Most High God.

We know how to humbly bow down, throwing our crowns at our master's holy feet in complete surrender before His throne, and we daily sing our victorious song!

We wave our love banner up high because we love with the agape love Jesus Christ does!

We are highly anointed, and we do not bow to foreign gods.

We do not compromise for success and popularity.

Our unconquerable spiritual quest is singleness of mind with a keen vision of heaven on high.

All forces of evil or foe cannot defeat our righteous cause because we obey our mighty Messiah with every God-given breath, and we will pass our heated pressure test and successfully run our swift race with our heavenly prize in sight!

All devils flee in terror at His living command and shed blood.

Friend, you can join this great army today. All you have to do is make Jesus the Lord of your life and wholly follow Him all your days.

When the battles around you are enflamed, just remember Jesus Christ has already won them all near and far. Friend, we know the world is full of troubles, but daily, we are triumphant in Christ our Lord.

The greatest army on earth needs no man-made gun in hand or military fatigues. It is larger than all the nations on Earth, and it's larger than life. Its commander sits on a royal throne, ruling the nations by the power of His Word. He is more than a prophet and more than a man; He is Jesus, the lamb of God; I AM that I AM.

His fight is of a supernatural force, and He is the greatest victor of all time.

The army of the Lord does not tolerate a pep-a-rally atmosphere, as we are at war with hostile principalities and powers on every imaginable front. We have the Word of God representations with the victorious Holy Ghost's power retaliations of supernatural proportions.

Look upon our hearts, O God! We desire to be the reflection of Jesus our Lord. Take full control of our hearts. Purge, burn, and consume our hearts and rotten flesh mess by Your all-consuming presence. We want to be a sweet-smelling fragrance before Your throne and not a stench in Your holy nostrils. We hate the flesh and its carnal enmity against You. We detest it, God. We hate the lust of the flesh and the pride of life and all carnal and wicked contaminates that are toxic to our souls.

Wake up the people, we pray, from the toxic drunken state of the world that they are in. We are desperate for revival in our hearts and lands. Deliver the sinful, sick souls by destroying all the darkness that is holding them captive. Shine Your light of truth right into their hearts and minds. In Jesus' name, we pray. Amen.

Romans 8:7 (KJV), "Because the carnal mind is enmity against God: for it is not subject to the law of God, neither indeed can be."

The army of the Lord has the mind of Christ, and we are fulfilling our designed destinies with the impacting force in the wisdom of God, embracing the unity of love for the body of Christ as a whole!

We must unify in love and join ranks in the spiritual war that we are all engaged in globally, riding out our destinies in the corporate mindset of being *one body* with many members!

Army of the Lord, embrace your kingdom identity realities in the force of faith every single day of your lives! Amen!

The sword of truth will never compromise but always rightly divide!

Romans 12:4–5 (KJV), "For as we have many members in one body, and all members have not the same office: So we, being many, are one body in Christ, and everyone members one of another."

Friend, in unity and the bond of peace as the body of Jesus and the army of God, we, the church, can accomplish more than we can think, fully imagine, or even dream. The power of unity is the power of the Trinity. As the heavenly Father, Jesus Christ, and the Holy Spirit are one, we are to be one in the body, and what a powerful force we could be against the forces of darkness.

The Lord spoke these words to me, "Be ruthless against the forces of hell."

We are the church. Let's show the world that we are serious about our mandate to dismantle hell's army by living holy before God's throne and demonstrating Jesus Christ's nature to all souls.

The White Horses of Revelation

We are dressed for battle twenty-four seven, 365 days against Lucifer and his demons.

Mount up, army. We are riding strong every day, empowered by the Word of the Lord and His Holy Spirit.

Friend, we must be rapture-ready.

Many years ago, I had a powerful encounter with the Lord that I want to share with an urgency in my heart: Prepare for your God now today. Don't delay, and don't turn Him away.

I was lying in my bed on my back, praying, when suddenly, the fiery glory of God started burning powerfully from the very soles of my feet upward as if a liquid fire was swiftly moving powerfully in my vessel. Then, the Holy Ghost opened my ears to hear this powerful and unforgettable sound from heaven that was astounding and wonderful indeed. The Lord allowed me in His tender mercies to hear the white horses of Revelation snorting and moving their hoofs back and forth continuously in movement, along with their nostrils snorting. They are in heaven, awaiting their set time to fulfill their arrival time on the earth, as recorded in Revelation 19:11.

I asked God the meaning of this supernatural encounter, and He said to me that the time is short, and we all must work quickly, as He told me He would do a quick work of the global harvesting of souls. He said that His liquid glory-fire will be the manifested and demonstrated glory that will burn in the hearts for the global revival. The holy fire power of a mighty outpouring will burn as upon the early church, and it will not be stopped by anything on the earth. His mighty army will wear the revival attire of holiness, and miracles will flood the earth. Also, great signs and wonders will be profound, and many will come forth trembling from their strongholds. The greatest move is yet to move among us.

It's time for all Christians to be in full attention before the throne of grace and align their hearts with heaven's mandates to go forth, dismantling hell's agendas at every turn! Amen!

> And he saith unto me, Write, Blessed are they which are called unto the marriage supper of the Lamb. And he saith unto me, These are the true sayings of God. And I fell at his feet to worship him. And he said unto me, See thou do it not: I am thy fellowservant, and of thy brethren that have the testimony of Jesus: worship God: for the testimony of Jesus is the spirit of prophecy. And I saw heaven opened, and behold a white horse; and he that sat upon him was called Faithful and True, and in righteousness he doth judge and make war. His eyes were as a flame of fire, and on his head were many crowns; and he had a name written, that no man knew, but he himself. And he was clothed with a vesture dipped in blood: and his name is called The Word of God. And the armies which were in heaven followed him upon white horses, clothed in fine linen, white and

clean. And out of his mouth goeth a sharp sword, that with it he should smite the nations: and he shall rule them with a rod of iron: and he treadeth the winepress of the fierceness and wrath of Almighty God. And he hath on his vesture and on his thigh a name written, KING OF KINGS, AND LORD OF LORDS.

Revelation 19:9–16 (KJV)

Friend, I also had another encounter back in the early 1980s. There was a most striking white horse running along a massive body of water, and its mane was gently blowing in the gentle breeze, as it was so effortlessly running in front of me. The setting was glorious as it was like a sandy beachfront, but the horse had no problems with the footing to run in the total liberty expression of heaven. I was so captivated by this encounter, and I asked the Lord about it because it was so glorious! I knew the white horse represented the white horses of Revelation, as Jesus rides on a white horse in Revelation 19. The Lord began speaking to me about my total liberty in Him and His Holy Spirit. He said that I was totally free from the spirit of religion, which faithfully protected me for decades, as I am deeply committed to *the Holy Bible* and not the leadings of the flesh.

The freedom expressions that I experienced in this encounter were so profound. God wants everyone free of anything that holds the heart captive. Hell has no hold on our lives and hearts. In Jesus' name!

Amos 3:7 (KJV), "Surely the Lord God will do nothing, but he revealeth his secret unto his servants the prophets."

My Gabriel Encounter

I love the Spirit of God and His Word, and I love living my life in the simplicity of the gospel of Jesus Christ and my simple child-like faith to choose to dream and choose to believe as I defy doubt, fear, and unbelief always!

Friend, choose to believe for what seems impossible, as God spoke these words to me many years ago. "He makes the impossible possible." I wanted to see the angel Gabriel, as God has shown me other angels as well. I prayed and I completely believed that God would allow me to have a visitation from him.

This powerful supernatural encounter occurred in a dream in the 1980s. I was standing outside in a driveway as darkness was upon the earth when the Spirit of the Lord began speaking to me to look up into the dark sky. To the left side of the sky came moving through the heavens a brilliant and striking red in color old Roman chariot that was trimmed out all around the edges with gold and inlaid with radiant jewels that also extended to the bridle of a white horse that was leading in front of the chariot. The horse had an exquisite golden bridle with many different colors of radiant jewels that matched the trim on the chariot. The wheels of the chariot were the old spoked wheels; they were gold and inlaid with the same jewels, and as with the trim of the chariot and bridle, it all matched.

I am so engulfed in the glory of God as I am watching this chariot and horse coming down out of the heavens toward me. It gently touched the earth in front of me and went past me about twenty feet or so. The back of the chariot was opened. I initially thought perhaps this was God the Father coming down to visit me. My child-like faith was just that, child-like!

The appearance of a man stepped out of the back of the chariot, turned toward me, and started my way. He didn't walk like we do as humans. He walked with a stately heavenly descent that was not of this world. As he stepped before me, he said, "Hi, Sherry. My name is Gabriel. I have been sent to you. Take an axe and chop until you can't chop no more." The battle axe….

I was so still and listened intently to the messenger angel. We shared more.

I asked if I could hug him, as I was so thankful for God allowing His angel to visit me and bring a word from His throne to me. When I did, he shook, and I asked the Lord what that meant. The Lord said, "Jesus Christ in Me embraced him." Jesus Christ is the glory of God, the creator! Amen.

Gabriel was dressed in a long white robe with a wide gold band around his waist. The neckline was a gold V-cut band. He had gold sandals on his feet. He had light color hair that was above his shoulders. His skin color was light in color. His face was like a shining glory, as I couldn't make out the exact profile and details of his face like we would make out the faces of humans.

This encounter was far more than just getting to see Angel Gabriel; it was a message and mandate from the holy one of Israel. It's for the end-time work that I must fulfill and help souls come up higher in the ways of the Spirit of God and His Holy Word.

Angel Gabriel stands in the presence of God. He is the messenger angel.

We are to never put and angel above God! We know they are ministering spirits, but all are under the authority of God. Amen. We always seek God the Holy Father, Jesus Christ the Son, and the Holy Spirit. Amen. There are times when angels are sent to people, as recorded in the Old and New Testaments. Note: Luke 1:26–38.

Gabriel is sent to Daniel, the prophet.

> And it came to pass, when I, even I Daniel, had seen the vision, and sought for the meaning, then, behold, there stood before me as the appearance of a man. And I heard a man's voice between the banks of Ulai, which called, and said, Gabriel, make this man to understand the vision.
>
> Daniel 8:15–16 (KJV)

Gabriel is sent to Zechariah, the father of John the Baptist.

Luke 1:19 (KJV), "And the angel answering said unto him, I am Gabriel, that stand in the presence of God; and am sent to speak unto thee, and to shew thee these glad tidings."

Many people crave the supernatural, but they get deceived by opening their hearts up to witchcraft and the tricks of Satan. See Deuteronomy 18.

Leviticus 19:31 (NLT), "Do not defile yourselves by turning to mediums or to those who consult the spirits of the dead. I am the Lord your God."

Jesus Christ loves you, and He died for you. He wants to reveal Himself powerfully to you, as He is no respecter of persons.

I invite you to say this Salvation Prayer:

Heavenly Father, I ask You to forgive me of all my sins, and I ask that You cleanse my heart from all unrighteousness. I ask Jesus Christ to come into my heart now and save me from Lucifer's hell, and I renounce all witchcraft practices. In Jesus' name, Amen. See John 3:16.

*Our bridegroom is coming back for His bride clothed in white linen, spotless and pure, so get ready, my friend, for the time is near.

Daniel 12:10 (KJV), "Many shall be purified, and made white, and tried; but the wicked shall do wickedly: and none of the wicked shall understand; but the wise shall understand."

Friend, I only pray that the words of this book have encouraged you to the highest and have helped you reach beyond yourself, taking hold of the greatness of God in all child-like faith where you, too, can live a life in the supernatural lifestyle of Jesus Christ with His Word being the rich balance of a just weight in the anointed flow of glory to glory. It's time to live in the fullness of Jesus Christ, where flesh is not dominant over the spirit, and the spirit of religion has no access to hinder your freedom in spirit and in truth. Amen.

God wants souls saved and set free and set on fire for His kingdom! In Jesus' name!

Share a smile, share a prayer, share the love of Jesus everywhere.

The End!

CLOSING THOUGHTS

You have a free-will choice to choose heaven or hell, faith or doubt.

Choose wisely because eternity is your forever future.

See John 3:16 and John 10:10. Jesus Christ yearns to save souls while the devil ruthlessly comes to destroy souls.

You can greatly soar into the supernatural kingdom identity realities with Jesus Christ (the blood covenant Word) leading the way. Only believe!

www.ingramcontent.com/pod-product-compliance
Lightning Source LLC
La Vergne TN
LVHW020731121224
798890LV00006B/151